Mr. Townsend & The Polish Prince

An American story of race, redemption and football

Mike Gastineau
with
Joe Purzycki

ISBN-13: 9781728922485

This book is dedicated to the memory of Nelson Townsend, a man of courage, vision and unlimited compassion.

And to Jeff Cannon, a gentle giant who often reminded us, "We are better off when we focus more on what we have in common than that which divides us."

To every young man who joined us on this journey, "We are the Hornets!"

ONE

The sun was trying to rise on a dreary November morning as Nelson Townsend trudged toward the jetway at Portland International Airport, pausing to extinguish his cigarette and ignoring the open newspaper on the counter. As long as his Saturday had been, this particular Sunday was going to be even longer.

United Airlines Flight 271 would be the first of three flights he would need to get home: down to San Francisco, over to Denver, connecting to Philadelphia. From there, he would gather his bags to make his way onto a bus for a 90-minute ride to Dover, Delaware.

The next 30 minutes would be tough since he couldn't smoke again until the plane reached cruising altitude. At that moment, he was upset about a lot of things, including the mere fact that he was smoking. He'd quit. Mostly. At least he'd promised his wife, Diane, he was quitting. But after what he'd witnessed Saturday night in Portland, he was going to need nicotine's help to get through the next few days. ("It was all I could do," he told Diane during his eventual mea culpa, "I'm ashamed to say they brought me to the point of smoking cigarettes.")

He had burned through several butts waiting at the gate and by the time he settled into his seat, he just wanted to be left alone.

If he was lucky, if all the legs on his cross-continent journey managed to avoid weather and gate delays, he might get home by 1 a.m. Monday. But only if he was lucky. And he wasn't counting on a lot of fortuitous bounces of the ball this weekend.

Working on a restless night didn't help, either, and Townsend knew full well that truly restful sleep was nowhere on the horizon.

Usually an approachable, affable sort, he stared straight ahead to avoid even casual eye contact. So naturally, the guy in the next seat nudged him, gesturing to an article in the *Oregonian* newspaper.

"Hey, look at this!" the guy said, chuckling, "Portland State beat some team a-hundred-and-five-to-nothin' last night."

This was not news to Townsend. He was the athletic director at Delaware State College, which was "some team" on the receiving end of the 15 touchdown beatdown. Townsend had watched every minute of the game along with 4,772 spectators at Civic Stadium who had thoroughly enjoyed the way the home team beat the living daylights out of his Hornets.

He'd watched a young Portland State quarterback named Neil Lomax toss seven touchdown passes ... *in the first quarter*. He cringed as he remembered the *sixteen* times Del State fumbled the football on a cold and rainy November night. And he still seethed as he recalled Portland State coach Darrel "Mouse" Davis sending his starters back into the game in the second half with a 63-point lead. By the end of the third quarter, the scoreboard read 98-0.

Final score: Portland State University 105. Delaware State College 0. It was the largest defeat in college football since 1936.

Townsend had company in his misery. The entire DSC team was on his flight and faced the same long journey home. As bad as it was for Townsend to watch, the game was even worse to play in, leaving Hornets players shell-shocked, drained emotionally, and incapable of feeling anything. They shared Townsend's desire to blend into the scenery and endure the interminable day and night of travel as inconspicuously as possible.

"When you travel as a team and you're in the airport, everyone wants to know who you are," said Matt Horace who played the entire game at right tackle. "I remember we didn't even want to say who we were or where we were from or what we'd been doing. It was so embarrassing and demoralizing."

The details of the game were fresh in Townsend's mind. And very last on his list of things to do was sharing small talk with the guy in the seat next to him, discussing the amazing game and its ramifications. He pretended not to hear as he stared out the window at the baggage handlers tossing cargo through the morning drizzle.

He was going to have to fire Charles Henderson, that much was certain. Henderson had been hired two years earlier to replace Ed Wyche, who had some success at DSC but was dismissed for using ineligible players. Wyche denied the allegation, but the story came unraveled when news surfaced that in one of the games in question an ineligible player caught two touchdown passes and was named the Mid-Eastern Athletic Conference (MEAC) player of the week. Later, Wyche dismissed the whole idea of sanctions against Delaware State in a *Delaware State News* story. "If you're on probation, you can't go on television. We're not going on TV. If you're on probation, you can't go to a bowl game. We're not going to a bowl game."

So, Henderson had been brought in, but that clearly wasn't working out, either. Which direction should Townsend take the Del State program? His eventual decision would surprise even himself.

When Townsend was hired in June of 1979, Del State football was, in fact, on probation by the NCAA, the NAIA, and the MEAC. "The only reason there wasn't more," he would say wryly, "is that there weren't any other governing bodies."

The team had won four games in 1979, but in 1980 Henderson's Hornets were getting drilled. Making things worse, the coaching staff reasoned that the losses were owing to a lack of toughness. According to Horace, the coaches would spend the week between games trying to change that.

"Coach Henderson's philosophy was 'how much pain can we inflict on you during the week to make you as tough as nails?'" the lineman recalled. "If you have a bad game on Saturday, then Monday is going to be hell. And Tuesday and Wednesday, too. And maybe, if you go through enough hell, you'll play better on Saturday."

But come Saturday, nobody seemed to play better, as Del State was clobbered by 39 points by Massachusetts, 52 by North Carolina A&T, 30 by Towson State, and 42 by Howard.

Townsend knew there had to be a better way. An athlete and lifelong educator, he had built a career as a teacher, counselor, vice-principal, coach, and administrator, who saw the value of sports, and this was not how he had envisioned those values bettering the lives of the student-athletes in his charge.

When he had been given the opportunity to step up to a Division I program from his alma mater at the University of Maryland Eastern Shore, he told the *State News*, "I think the athletic program at Delaware State is a gold mine. They just need someone to come in, roll up his sleeves, and get the work done. I can do that."

And the winter of 1980-81 was clearly a pivotal moment in his career and the life of DSC athletics.

Dr. Luna Mishoe, the president of the college, knew as much. Dr. Mishoe was a popular leader in Dover. He oversaw continued growth and guided the school through turbulent anti-war and civil rights protests (including a National Guard response) in 1968. Under Dr. Mishoe, the school's accreditation was reaffirmed four times; by the late 1970s, DSC's school leaders saw athletics as an appropriate way to show its general wherewithal. The Del State administration decided to join other MEAC schools jumping from Division II to Division I. Dr. Mishoe had hired Townsend to oversee the move.

While Townsend's plane sat on a tarmac on the West Coast, Dr. Mishoe was at his home in Dover wondering about the result of the game. There had been no live radio or TV coverage and the game ended too late for the score to be reported by Eastern newspapers. At noon he got a call from sportswriter Scott Wasser of the *State News*.

"I wanted to talk to you about last night's game," Wasser said.

"Oh, I'm glad you called," Dr. Mishoe replied. "I didn't hear anything about it. Did you get the score? Did we win?"

"Well, uh, no. In fact, you're going to be stunned."

When Wasser relayed the news, there was an uncomfortably long silence on the line.

"Are you kidding?" Dr. Mishoe finally said. "Are you joking with me?"

"No, Dr. Mishoe, I'm not," Wasser said, almost apologizing. "I wouldn't joke about something like that." After another long pause, Wasser asked if Dr. Mishoe had a comment for the paper.

"I can't tell you anything right now," the president said. "I've got to find out more about what happened. I'll call you back."

Word was slowly getting out and soon even Brent Musburger and Irv Cross were talking about it on CBS on *The NFL Today*: "Get a load of this, folks," Musburger said as Cross laughed. "This is no joke. Last night in Portland, Delaware State lost to Portland State 105 to 0." The game's result also was featured on the new all-sports channel ESPN with similar chortling and guffaws.

Dr. Mishoe believed that a school president should handle the academic and business side of a college while letting the athletic administration handle sports, and he felt he had the right man to do that in Townsend. But DSC was largely dependent on funding from the Delaware state government, and a loss this dramatic was bound to raise eyebrows across town at the state house.

Mishoe knew he'd soon be getting calls from legislators who would want to know what happened to the football team in Portland. He wanted to know the same thing.

"One hundred and five ..." the guy in the seat next to Townsend said incredulously, louder this time. Was that an elbow nudge or just his seatmate shifting in his seat? *"To nothing!* You see this? Portland State beat Delaware State 105 to zip last night. That offense Mouse Davis is running is space-age stuff, man. A hundred and five points. Imagine that!"

The stranger was smiling as he offered the paper to Townsend, who couldn't ignore the well-intentioned intrusion any longer. So, the athletic director at Delaware State College made a quick decision that he hoped would allow him some peace and quiet for the rest of the flight.

"105 to nothing?! Are you kidding me?" he asked in a voice tinged with disbelief. "Let me see that." He quickly scanned the story, throwing in an "unbelievable" here and a "wow" there. Promptly, he gave the paper back with a well-timed, "huh." He never let on who he was or what he knew.

Townsend was a proud man who had already accomplished a great deal in his life. But on this day, it was easier and less painful to just pretend he was someone else.

TWO

Whthen Townsend walked into Mishoe's office Monday morning two newspapers were pointedly side-by-side on the conference table.

Del State President Launches Probe After Record Loss
– *Delaware State News*

Humiliated Del State President Will Probe Program
– *Wilmington News Journal*

Both papers contained quotes that indicated everyone involved understood the severity of the situation.

"To tell you the truth, this is the most humiliating thing I've ever heard in my life," Dr. Mishoe said. "The score indicates to me that there looks like there was no effort on our part. Everything is askew right now."

Board of Trustees President William G. Dix bluntly declared that "no team should be that poor."

"My reaction is one of incredulity," said board member and Dover attorney Richard Barros. "I feel we have a good man in Mr. Townsend, but I don't know much about Henderson. A losing season is not a disaster but when you get beat 105-to-0 there's a deep problem." Barros added the board was "obligated" to investigate the program in the wake of the defeat.

At least the football coach was straightforward when asked about his future. "My status?" Henderson said, responding to a reporter's question. "It's shaky."

That status and the surrounding issues were taking up entirely too much of Mishoe's time: The Board of Trustees was planning to investigate, state legislators were burning up his phone line, well-meaning friends were pestering him to find out what was happening. The college president was already fed up with it.

"I think we should fire Henderson immediately," is how he opened his meeting with Townsend. The athletic director agreed that the coaching change had to be made, but he thought doing so with two games left in the season would be a disservice to the team. "Let's let him finish the season," Townsend suggested, "and then evaluate the program like we've planned all along."

Townsend calmed Dr. Mishoe, who agreed to wait two weeks before making a final decision – or at least making it public. "We have a responsibility to question things when we think they're way off," the college president told reporters later in the day. "But the athletic director must make the final decision. The board can discuss it and do what it wants to do but my recommendation is that we follow the advice of our AD and handle this professionally."

Townsend knew some would question his decision, but felt continuity was the best thing for the football team. "At the heart of any decision I make is the consideration of the athlete. I don't care about the popularity of my decisions. I care about the athletes."

Mishoe and Townsend weren't the only one facing reporters that day. Pat "Thunder" Thornton, who played several positions on both sides of the ball during his Del State career, remembers the entire week being filled with the kind of media distractions the team usually didn't have. The huge loss had turned the Hornets into both a punch line and a punching bag for the media.

"You would have thought we had won the national champion-ship," Thornton said, "with all the reporters who wanted to talk to us about the Portland game." When he and his teammates weren't explaining the loss to the media, they were engaged in a brutal week of practice.

"Our coaches had us beat the hell out of each other in the pits. One on one. Two on one. Three on one. I never experienced a week like that before. A lot of us got injured. It was rock bottom for the program."

Amazingly, the team pulled together and posted a surprising win over Central State. But the final week of the season found them on the wrong end of a 57-9 drubbing at Florida A&M. Two weeks later, at a meeting when the Board of Trustees was planning to fire him, Henderson turned in his resignation.

At that meeting, Townsend proposed that the school change the structure of the coaching staff. Henderson had seven assistant coaches but only two of them worked full-time. Townsend's plan was to budget for five assistants who would be full-time employees of the athletic department.

He proposed finishing the remodel of Alumni Stadium to include better locker room facilities, increasing the budget for weight training equipment, and establishing a training table for athletes to ensure better nutrition.

"If we continue with the same program it cannot exist like this," said trustee Barros, who along with the other board members agreed with Townsend's ideas. "Even if we dropped back to Division II or Division III we would have the same problems. We have to revamp the entire program."

The trustees empowered Townsend to form a search committee to make a recommendation to the school's athletic council, an 11-member group made up of administrators, faculty, and students. The athletic council would likely approve the recommendation and send it to the Board of Trustees for the final decision.

Townsend said his committee would be looking for three things in the new head coach: "I'm looking for someone with proven leadership abilities, someone who can organize and operate our program at a professional level, and someone who can recruit." He said concerns about Henderson's recruiting ability in the wake of the Portland State loss was the primary reason he wanted a new coach.

"It would have been very difficult for Coach Henderson to walk up to a young man and say, 'We want to recruit you after a loss that got more national attention than if we had launched a rocket here on campus.'"

It's been said that the football program is the front porch of most universities. It's not the most important thing, but it's often the first thing people see. And by the end of the 1980 season, DSC's front porch needed massive repairs. Yet, the makeover Nelson Townsend was about to propose would send shockwaves through Delaware State College, the Historically Black College and Universities (HBCUs) community, and the sports world.

THREE

T he way the program was staggering at the end of 1980 didn't deter a long list of candidates who were interested in becoming the next head football coach at Delaware State College.

After all, there were only 183 people in the United States who had the job of Division I head football coach (138 in I-A, 45 in I-AA). Coaches' salaries had not yet exploded, but if you had a Division I job you were able to make a comfortable living.

The list included Billy Joe, who quickly emerged as the favorite in the DSC community, having played football at Villanova and in the NFL, even winning a Super Bowl with the New York Jets. He spent seven years as head coach at Cheyney State (a Division II school in Pennsylvania), and then became offensive backfield coach for the Philadelphia Eagles in 1979. Thanks to Dover's proximity to Philadelphia, players at Del State knew his name and were excited about the possibility of playing for a guy who had played and coached in the NFL.

Also interested was Bob Andrus, a successful head coach in town at the high school and junior college levels. Following a great run at Dover High, which included a 29-game winning streak, Andrus was amid a 14-year stretch at Wesley College in Dover. He had won four conference titles and in 1976 his 10-0 team was the second-ranked junior college program in America.

Then there was Joe Purzycki.

Although Purzycki didn't have the credentials of some candidates, he had name recognition in Delaware. He had been a three-year starting cornerback and captain for Tubby Raymond's powerful University of Delaware program and was an honorable mention AP

All-American in 1969 when he led the country with nine interceptions. Purzycki had spent six years coaching high school football in Delaware, including three wildly successful seasons at Caesar Rodney High School outside Dover where his teams went 33-2 and won the 1975 state championship.

In 1978, the already legendary Raymond hired Purzycki to be the secondary coach at Delaware. The Blue Hens went 32-7 in the three years Purzycki was on the staff, winning the Division II championship in 1979. By 1980, the program had jumped into Division I-AA and finished the season 9-2.

As the Blue Hen staff began off-season recruiting, Purzycki felt he had reached a professional crossroads. Jumping from high school to UD to work with Raymond put him in the brighter spotlight of college football, but he was anxious to run his own program again. He considered himself a head coach, and beside his professional ambition, Purzycki needed the money that only a head position offered then.

He and his wife Sharon had two children and wanted more. He was just 33 years old, but after more than a decade in coaching, he was making just $12,500 as the defensive backs coach at Delaware. He couldn't help but consider options outside of football, and while investigating a career in law enforcement, he scored well on the FBI exam. But the timing for that move couldn't have been worse. Ronald Reagan had won the 1980 presidential election promising smaller government and speculation held that he would issue a federal hiring freeze – which he did within days of taking office. The FBI was not going to be a viable option anytime soon.

Purzycki was sitting at his desk one afternoon pondering his limited options when his phone rang.

Jack Ireland was a newspaper reporter who had covered sports in Delaware for more than a decade, first for the *Seaford Leader* then for the *Wilmington News Journal*. He had covered Purzycki's stint as head coach at Woodbridge High School, his run at Caesar Rodney High School, and the return to his alma mater as an assistant. They were the same age and had spent a lot of time together. So, Purzycki wasn't surprised when he heard Ireland's voice on the other end of the line. The surprise came in Ireland's first question.

"Can we talk off the record?"

In the reporter/coach relationship that question usually goes in the other direction. But here was Ireland asking Purzycki in advance to keep their conversation just between them.

"Sure," Purzycki responded.

"Nelson Townsend called me and asked me to reach out to you to see if you have any interest in the Delaware State job," Ireland said.

The Delaware State opening had been a topic of conversation around the University of Delaware football office, but the tone was usually one of sympathy. Coaches shook their heads in disbelief as they talked about the Portland State game, the still-recent scandal involving ineligible players, and the sorry state of the overall program.

Purzycki knew a lot about the Del State program. Like many, he believed the school could be doing a lot more with football. But there was more to it than that.

"Jack, I'd actually consider it,' Purzycki said, "but they'll never hire a white coach. I've been told that by a lot of people."

Ireland had heard the same thing. DSC often interviewed white candidates for coaching jobs but did not hire them. At the time, only two black men held head coaching positions in college football programs outside the network of Historic Black Colleges and Universities, so it was easy to understand Del State's desire to hire black coaches.

Ireland knew Purzycki wanted to be a head coach and he knew he was good. He had watched him steamroll his way to 33 wins at Caesar Rodney in one of the greatest three-year stretches in Delaware history. Just as significant, he was convinced big changes were coming at DSC.

"I think Nelson is serious about it this time," he said. "They have to do something dramatic. They're under a lot of pressure from the state legislature after everything that's gone on there in the past decade. Townsend, Dr. Mishoe, and the trustees all feel like they've got to do something to get the program going."

Purzycki was intrigued but still skeptical. "I don't want to hurt my reputation with Tubby and be chasing something unless they are dead serious."

"Call him, have a conversation, and decide for yourself," Ireland said. "But I'm telling you, things are different this time."

Purzycki couldn't dismiss the thought. He wanted to be a head coach. He wanted to lead a team. He saw that at DSC, there was nowhere to go but up.

He also knew that on all levels, this was a long shot. But it was a shot. "I was still dubious," he said later. "One conversation with Jack Ireland didn't completely change my mind about what I thought was the likely outcome for me at Del State. But I decided to call Nelson anyway."

When Purzycki called, it didn't take long for Townsend to cut through the small talk to ask him about his interest in the job. Purzycki felt it was important to be completely honest from the start.

"Are you serious about this?" he asked. "Because I can't hurt my reputation with Tubby unless you're actually considering me as a candidate and not just someone to be interviewed."

Townsend countered Purzycki's direct question with a direct question of his own.

"Are YOU serious? Because I can't put my neck on the line if you're not serious. I don't want you to use me for leverage with Tubby."

It was a shrewd move. Purzycki's concerns were real, but Townsend had even more at stake. Purzycki gauged Townsend's response and quickly realized this was a situation worth exploring.

"No, no, no. I'm not using this as any leverage," he responded. "I'm serious about it as long as I'm not being used as just a white candidate."

"I promise you're not," Townsend replied. "Why don't you come down to Dover and we'll talk."

Purzycki was now obligated to tell his boss about the conversation. Partially because he didn't want to tip his hand at how interested he was in the job, and partially because he still harbored some skepticism even after talking to Townsend, he downplayed the situation to Raymond. He said he thought Del State wanted to talk to him primarily because of his six years as a high school head coach in southern Delaware. Raymond saw the benefits as limited.

"Go talk to them. It will be a good experience," Raymond offered, before adding, "but you'd be crazy to ever go there."

A few days later, Purzycki drove to Dover and met with Townsend. The two men quickly realized they had strong chemistry. "We liked each other from the start," Purzycki said.

In discussing their families and backgrounds, they found they shared many personality traits. Purzycki was from the city and Townsend from the country but both had grown up in loving homes with a very strong parental presence. Each was comfortable being himself: gregarious, quick to laugh, and almost instantly of similar mind with the other. Neither had time for bullshit. Before long, they were discussing how to get Delaware State out of its mess.

Townsend told Purzycki that Delaware State was ready to invest in the program. He had worked with the college's trustees to preload many of the anticipated improvements that any quality candidate would insist on. The coaching staff was already being restructured to turn assistants into full-time employees with benefits. The recruiting budget would increase, the 40 scholarships would grow to 60 – still below the maximum of 75 in Division I-AA, but a step in the right direction.

Townsend took Purzycki for a walk across campus on a chilly winter afternoon. They arrived at the weight room and the candidate was shocked by the meager offerings – a universal gym, a couple sets of barbells, and a bench. One bench. Purzycki gasped, "Any high school in the state of Delaware has a better weight room," and Townsend could only laugh in agreement.

This, too, was an example of tangible progress for the program under a new head coach, Townsend pointed out, noting that when he was hired as athletic director, the entire "weight training facility" consisted of a single bar with a couple hundred pounds of weights. The bar and weights resided outdoors under the bleachers of the stadium in a pile of weeds. Some of the equipment had begun to rust.

Yes, there was room to grow at Del State. Purzycki wondered aloud what the room was being used for before Townsend moved in the school's small stock of weights.

"For many years, this is where visiting teams stayed when they played Delaware State," Townsend related. "The players slept in here on cots."

Until the late 1970s, visiting teams couldn't be guaranteed space in hotel rooms in many towns, including Dover. Throughout the MEAC and other leagues with HBCUs, it was standard procedure for the home team to provide some sort of sleeping arrangements for their guests. Visiting teams generally ate in the host school's dining hall, too, since they couldn't always get served in area restaurants.

The two men left the weight room and took a short drive to the back of campus, where Townsend pointed to a development of about 30 houses.

"Those houses are faculty housing," he told Purzycki. "In the '50s and '60s, it was difficult for our teachers to find quality housing in Dover. The college purchased these homes, so they would have a place to live."

Purzycki knew that there were inequities in the world that created difficult circumstances for black Americans, but in all his years traveling for football as a player and as a coach, he'd never even considered the notion of a team not being allowed to sleep in a hotel or eat in a restaurant. He had never worried about not being able to find a decent home for his family due to his skin color.

The idea of a group of young men sleeping on cots the night before a game created a stark, unshakable image in his mind. The idea of a college teacher being denied adequate housing was a level of discrimination utterly foreign to him, and his reaction was emotional and visceral.

He was starting to realize that taking the job at Delaware State would inject him into a different world from the one he'd been living and working in. He'd be taking on football challenges, financial challenges, and societal challenges that he understood existed but never had to face. Townsend wanted to be sure that Purzycki had a clear understanding of what he was getting into.

"Your biggest problem is this: you're going to find out what it's like to be in the minority. It's *you* who's going to have to see everybody else's side of things. And I can tell you right now it's not going to be easy. A lot of the people who work here have scars from years of segregation. Many of them had to attend all-black high schools. A lot of the faculty here know nothing but Delaware State College as both their college experience and their work experience. They're not going to be open to the idea of a white coach."

Townsend foresaw another potential problem he wanted Purzycki to think about. Outside the network of HBCUs, only two schools had African-American head coaches in 1981 (Willie Jeffries at Wichita

State and Dennis Green at Northwestern). Townsend knew that would become an issue if he hired Purzycki.

"The other schools in our conference are all HBCUs, as are most of the schools we play in football. There are people who are not going to be happy with a white man taking a leadership position at Delaware State College."

Purzycki started to interrupt to ask why Townsend would even consider such a step when the athletic director challenged him by saying he knew Purzycki was tough but wondered if he was tough enough to work in an environment where his every move would be severely scrutinized.

And then he told him why he was pursuing him as a prime candidate: "You played at and you coach at one of the great programs in the country. I need you to take that model of Delaware football that has made you successful and come down here and teach us how to build that kind of program."

Townsend told him he was one of three candidates that would be interviewed. Purzycki's original hesitancy about whether Townsend and Delaware State would really consider hiring him was fading to zero. As he shook hands with Townsend any lingering feelings he had about the sincerity of the DSC athletic director had disappeared. He was a candidate for the job. And if he was reading the situation correctly, he was the top candidate.

FOUR

"One thing I knew after that first day with Nelson," Purzycki remembered, "is that we trusted each other. That was going to be very important if this was going to work. You look in a man's eyes and you make a judgment. We believed in each other right away."

Townsend had indicated that the process was going to move quickly and Purzycki realized it was time to come clean with his boss at Delaware. News that he was a candidate for the Del State job would come out soon enough and as tough as the conversation was going to be, it would be better if Raymond heard it from him rather than from the rumor mill or the newspaper.

Even though Raymond himself had looked at other jobs, and recently spent time flirting with Syracuse about its opening, he was not happy when Purzycki told him that he was going to interview at Del State and that he had the feeling he was a top candidate.

"Tubby thought Delaware football was the center of the universe and why would you ever leave Camelot?" Purzycki said. "When people did leave, he didn't understand why." Purzycki explained his desire to be a head coach. He felt he needed to run his own team and his heart wasn't in being an assistant coach.

"You're writing your own professional epitaph," Raymond warned. "I'm not worried about the people you can reach to work with you, but there are people you won't be able to reach and that's what's going to undermine you." Purzycki had tremendous respect for the Blue Hens head coach but felt it was somewhat ironic that he was discouraging him from pursuing the job.

"I decided to get into coaching because of Tubby. He was the greatest influence on my life outside of my father. During my junior year of college, I started seriously thinking about what I wanted to do. I spent a lot of time watching him and I started to think coaching was something I could do and something I wanted to do. I was always a natural leader and having a team to coach was really appealing to me."

Purzycki's cards were now on the table and although he wanted Raymond's support he was ready to pursue the job with or without it. Raymond's reaction gave him an uneasy mixture of emotions. He was saddened that he would have to move forward without his mentor's help, but Raymond's reaction fueled him. He became defiant and dug in to pursue the job.

Not having Raymond on his team meant he would have to get support from Raymond's boss, athletic director Dave Nelson. Nelson was the former head football coach at Delaware and the man who originally brought to the school the famed Wing-T offense from Michigan. Nelson was willing to write a letter to Townsend on Purzycki's behalf, but he had one caveat.

"I am not going to recommend you unless you take this job if it's offered," he told Purzycki. "You give me your word that you'll take it if they offer it and I'll send the letter." Purzycki assured him that was the case and Nelson followed through.

In the last week of December, Purzycki had another series of meetings in Dover with Townsend and three members of the school's search committee: Dr. Richard Wynder, Allen Hamilton, and June McGuire. He was confident enough about getting an offer that he began thinking about assembling a staff. His first discussion regarding that was with Herky Billings.

Like Purzycki, Billings had played and was now the receivers coach at Delaware. He had been a decorated high school player on legendary teams at Middletown High School and had been a halfback for Tubby Raymond from 1972 to 1974. He would be a great fit for Purzycki's plan for a variety of reasons.

First, he was a football junkie. He loved to talk, teach, and watch football. If ever someone had been born to coach, Purzycki felt, it was Herky.

Second, he had spent a lot of time in Delaware and even though he knew about all the problems at Del State, he was optimistic about what could be done in Dover. "Del State had always been a stepchild in the state compared to Delaware," Billings said. "But I thought they had great potential and I always thought they deserved a better chance than they had been given."

Purzycki knew he faced a massive job and thought Billings' can-do optimism was imperative. "He kept telling me, 'Joe, that place is a sleeping giant.'" During one of their conversations, Purzycki wondered about others who might be a good fit on the potential staff, which allowed his budding offensive coordinator to weigh in.

"You should talk to Bill Collick."

Collick was a Lewes, Delaware, native who had played at Wesley College in Dover for two years. He then transferred to Delaware where he didn't play football but earned his degree. He had returned to his hometown and was an assistant coach at Cape Henlopen High School.

Purzycki felt one of the keys to building sustained success at DSC was to recruit locally. To do that successfully, he needed to find a high school coach from Delaware who had credibility. "There is not a finer human being who walks the face of the earth than Bill," Billings said. "He's from here. He's got a good name among the coaching and football community. He'd be perfect for what you're trying to do."

Purzycki contacted Collick and found that he shared Billings' attitude that good things could be done at Delaware State. Collick's connection to the school was personal (his uncle Carl was a DSC graduate) and he was excited about the potential to work there.

Purzycki asked both guys to keep the conversations private since there was no official word yet that he was even a candidate for the job. That word was coming soon enough. And once that happened Tubby Raymond wasn't the only person unhappy about it.

On the first Monday of 1981, Nelson Townsend announced that interviews with candidates were complete and that he planned to have a coach in place by the end of the week (Friday, January 9th). The annual MEAC winter meetings in Daytona Beach, Florida, were scheduled for that weekend and he expected to have hired a coach by then.

Townsend's search committee had narrowed the field to a short list and he outlined the week ahead for reporters: Tuesday night, he would present his choice to the athletic council, which included DSC President Luna Mishoe. Thursday, Dr. Mishoe would take the final recommendation to the school's trustees for final approval. If everything went according to plan, the school would announce the new coach on Friday morning and by Friday afternoon Townsend would be off to Florida.

"I thought that I'd be back in Dover on Thursday night to be interviewed by the trustees," Purzycki said. "It was my belief that whoever they interviewed first was their first choice as long as the interview went well. If it didn't go well, they'd move on to other choices."

In a Tuesday story by Jack Ireland in the *News Journal*, Purzycki spoke like a man who knew he had a good shot at the job.

"I know everybody that applied probably said what a great challenge it would be," Purzycki said. "I see the job a little differently. I think Delaware State can have a viable football program if given the time to develop. I guess I don't sound too humble, but I think the program needs somebody who can really get the entire state and local community behind it. I feel in the positions I've had with the people of this state, I'm the best person to sell the Delaware State program. It's a challenge and I want to be with a program with a future."

But on the same day, Scott Wasser wrote a column for the *Delaware State News* starting with a declaration that opened eyes all over the First State.

> *"There's a good chance Delaware State College will have a new head football coach by this weekend. There's a good chance that coach will be white. Please don't look for any hidden meaning between those first two lines. There is none. I'm simply stating facts."*

Wasser wrote that of the 10 original finalists for the job only three were black. Two of those were assistant coaches to Clarence Henderson and Ed Wyche, and given the state of the program, it was unlikely that either Jackie Robinson or Roy White would be hired. That meant Billy Joe was the only serious black candidate.

Wasser pointed out that Billy Joe was the ideal candidate. Delaware State's team was primarily black. The Hornets played in a conference comprised of HBCUs and most of their non-conference games were scheduled against the same. Joe had been a head coach, he was currently an assistant with the Super Bowl-bound Eagles. It was logical to assume that he would be the choice.

Wasser then dropped this bomb: *"At the risk of sounding like a bigot, however, I hope the new Del State coach is white."*

Wasser detailed the long list of problems and embarrassments tied to Del State football in the past decade. He suggested that all those problems created a situation where a dramatic change was needed to ensure the program would garner respect from and for the community it represented. He pointed out that making fun of Delaware State football was a popular pastime among local sports fans and that hiring a white coach would be the *"kind of dramatic change it will take to wake up people in this area to the fact that Del State's administration really is trying to turn things around. Maybe that's the kind of change it takes to make people stop pointing their fingers and snickering every time some well-intentioned plan backfires at Del State."*

Wasser admits that he hoped the column would get people thinking and talking about the topic, as any good column would.

"But, I also believed it," Wasser said. "The program was in such shambles and it was such a joke and a laughingstock. I just felt like that would be such a dramatic and striking change that it would set the tone that they were serious about being respectable if not good. It had nothing to do with white and black. To my mind, that was the most striking and distinctive thing they could do to make it clear that this was a different ball game. I felt there was a real chance they were going to hire a white coach, which would have been unthinkable two years earlier."

Wasser's column indeed precipitated a lot of conversation among athletes, students, faculty, and administrators. And for Townsend, it effectively short-circuited his opportunity to explain his process and thinking to the athletic council as well as the Board of Trustees.

The columnist wasn't surprised when the athletic director called him after his column ran. The two men had a good working relationship, but as Townsend told Wasser, "You didn't help me out by writing this column. There are people in the administration here who are not going to react well to an outsider telling them what to do. It was going to be a tough sell to start with … and now…"

Well, now Townsend's new coach had become controversial even before he was hired.

Some of the members of the board were downright angry. People throughout the DSC community took umbrage that a white newspaper columnist was implying that hiring a black coach might lead to more problems for the beleaguered football program. Wasser's opinion was commonly received as ONLY hiring a white coach could right the ship.

School officials had already decided that the new coach, whoever he was, would get more support than previous coaches. Plans for the new weight room, new locker room, full-time assistant coaches, and even the 50-percent increase in scholarship athletes had been discussed publicly. Some people on the DSC campus wondered aloud if those changes could have benefitted Charles Henderson. Now, Henderson was gone, and if Wasser was right, the guy who would get to take advantage of all these upgrades would be white. That perspective began to generate serious heat and debate on campus.

Several members of the Board of Trustees felt that heat and decided to put the brakes on Townsend's timeframe for hiring the new coach. They told him that how the plan was executed would be their choice, not his. Rather than Townsend sending one candidate, they preferred to interview three finalists. "We need some rationale if we do make the choice to hire Purzycki," one board member told Townsend, "other than just 'he's your guy.'"

Townsend presented his list of candidates to the athletic council on Thursday (two days later than he originally planned) and told Wasser in a story published on Sunday, January 11th, that the process of finding a new coach was going to take more time. That's when it became apparent that a rift had developed between Townsend and others at the university who preferred Billy Joe.

Townsend's job was further complicated when news leaked out that his search committee had been asked to interview a "mystery candidate" on January 12th. That interview was set up by James Hardcastle, a member of the athletic council and the board of trustees. The new candidate turned out to be North Carolina A&T coach Jim McKinley. His Aggies had won nine games the previous season, including 52-0 over Del State.

Also, a story in the *News Journal* about Billy Joe – who along with the rest of the Eagles coaching staff was preparing for the Super Bowl after Philadelphia had defeated Dallas to win the NFC title – ramped up the drama further. "I still haven't heard a thing about the job and I thought I might have a good chance of getting it," Joe told Ireland. "I would love to have the job and I can't understand why someone hasn't been named by now."

He wasn't the only candidate wondering what was happening. "I only knew what I was reading in the paper," Purzycki remembered. One time, he reached out to Townsend who assured him everything was still on track.

"You are my guy," Townsend told him, "but you've got to hang in there. I've gotta work through this."

The main reason no one had the job yet was that the athletic council did not agree with Townsend and his search committee, who had listed Purzycki as the top choice, with Joe second and McKinley third. The athletic council had Joe as the man for the job, with McKinley as the second choice and Purzycki third. Further complicating things was that athletic council chairman Allen Hamilton agreed with Townsend that Purzycki should be the top choice. Hamilton confirmed that there was no small amount of chaos in the ongoing search: "It's obvious I'm not satisfied with the athletic council's recommendation. But, I've got to take the Fifth Amendment right now concerning who that choice is. And if the trustees don't like our choice, they can always change their mind."

The Board of Trustees thought they would be getting one list recommending a new coach. Instead, the search committee and the athletic council submitted separate lists in letters dated January 13th.

There was speculation that while Joe and Purzycki legitimately wanted the job, McKinley was using the Del State opening as leverage in his negotiations for a new deal at North Carolina A&T. That idea was confirmed in a letter Dr. Mishoe sent to the trustees on January 14th. In the letter, Mishoe reported that McKinley had called him the previous evening and informed him that if he were to be selected as the new coach he would require the school to hire his top four assistant coaches from his current job and have them on the payroll starting on March 1st.

This meant McKinley was taking himself out of the running, since it was understood that Delaware State did not have money budgeted for new assistant coaches until the next fiscal year (starting July 1st) and the new coach would work as a staff of one until that date. McKinley remained as a finalist, but the school was not going to be able to meet his demands.

A week after Townsend originally planned to have things wrapped up, the process finally appeared to be moving to a conclusion. Townsend and Hamilton wanted Purzycki, a majority of the athletic council wanted Joe, and the trustees would decide. But Mishoe cautioned anyone who thought that the final decision would be made quickly: "The trustees are being notified of the decisions (of the search committee and the athletic council) by mail and the way the mail is they may not be notified for a couple days."

Eventually, the mail got delivered and the trustees had to choose. On January 20th, while the country was celebrating the inauguration of Ronald Reagan, Purzycki got a call from Townsend.

"The board of trustees wants to interview you tomorrow night," Townsend said. "You'll be the first candidate interviewed and if it goes well, you'll get the job."

Purzycki left his home the next day around dusk for the one-hour trip to Dover. As he drove, he continually went over answers in his head to the questions he expected to hear. He also worried about what, exactly, to expect. He'd watched the story unfold as a football soap opera for the past several weeks and couldn't help but speculate that there might still be more surprises.

Purzycki parked his car and as he walked into the building to meet Townsend, he bumped into a custodian who had been friendly to him during his first two visits to campus.

"You gotta relax coach!" he boomed. "You the man!"

Buoyed by that quick shot of confidence he walked into Townsend's office. The athletic director greeted him nervously and Purzycki immediately realized something was wrong.

"You're going to have to wait here for a few minutes," Townsend said. "I'll have somebody come to get you and bring you to the library when the trustees are ready to meet with you. We've had a little change in plans and some of the other candidates are on campus."

Townsend noticed the crestfallen look on the face of the man he wanted to get the job. "Relax, Joe. It's going be OK."

Townsend left the office but promised Purzycki it wouldn't be long before someone came to get him. As he sat alone in Townsend's office, for the first time in the weeks since things had gotten serious, he had a sobering realization. "OK ... maybe I'm not the man."

FIVE

Finally, Purzycki's escort arrived and they took the short walk between buildings on a chilly night. When they opened the door to the library the first thing Purzycki saw was Jack Ireland talking to someone on a pay phone.

"That's odd," Purzycki thought to himself. "What's Jack doing here? And why are there other reporters and TV cameras here? Surely this is not for me."

He was right. As he reached the top of a flight of stairs to the second floor, he saw Billy Joe walking out of the meeting room, smiling and shaking hands with people.

The Eagles were getting ready to play Oakland in Super Bowl XV, yet Joe had flown up from New Orleans to meet with the trustees. There were plenty of Eagles fans at DSC and Joe's presence four days before the big game explained the buzz in the building.

"Good God," Purzycki muttered to himself. Townsend had indicated to Purzycki all along that the first person interviewed was likely to be the first choice to be the new coach, and now he was seeing that Billy Joe had been given the first interview with the board. Suddenly he felt very much like a superfluous candidate. He had little choice but to shake off his surprise and do the best he could with the trustees.

"They ushered Billy out and they ushered me in with no explanation," he said. "I quickly decided not to bring it up. I was a little shocked to see him and to realize he had gotten the first interview but bringing that up would have meant confronting Nelson in front of the entire room, and I knew that wasn't a good idea."

(Although he didn't know it at the time, Purzycki wasn't even the second person interviewed. McKinley had been first in with the trustees late in the afternoon. Joe was next, and Purzycki was the last of the three.)

But quickly, trustee Richard Barros soothed Purzycki's rattled nerves with some early questions ("He asked me 12 or 13 in rapid-fire succession and I could tell by his tone that he was on my side," Purzycki said.) and it wasn't long before the coach was comfortably explaining his vision for the future of Delaware State College football.

He presented each member of the board with a laminated 20-page booklet in the school's colors of blue and red detailing his plan.

He articulated his philosophy of recruiting ("You don't recruit just a player, you recruit his family.").

He described the discipline necessary to keep kids in school and eligible to play.

He explained how he would set up study halls and academic support so that players could succeed off the field as well as on.

He discussed how and why he wanted to redshirt almost all freshman, so he could eventually have a team that leaned on experienced players.

He laid out his offense and defense, which incidentally, had been successful for years.

He detailed the program's progression – of two wins in his first year, four in his second, six in his third and, significantly, eight in his fourth.

When Purzycki exited an hour later, Townsend approached him and said softly, "Joe, I'll call you later." Purzycki recognized that Townsend was telling him that he knew things hadn't unfolded the way he told him they would. As he made his way out of the DSC campus toward the freeway he was certain of two things:

1) "Everything clicked – I knew I had nailed the interview."
2) "There was no way I was getting the job. Billy Joe walked out of his interview and the students and players were all over him. When I walked out of the same room an hour later nobody came near me. Nobody acknowledged me."

In the meantime, Allen Hamilton stood in the meeting room and implored the others to join him in supporting Purzycki. As chairman of the athletic council, he explained why he felt this young coach from UD was the best man for the job, and he just happened to be white. Hamilton knew the game. He was a running back for East Orange High School in the 1950s (where he was teammates with actor John Amos) and was good enough to get a scholarship from Rutgers. An injury there derailed his career, and he subsequently transferred to Delaware State. He had been a math major and eventually was hired by the school to lead the mathematics department.

"The other guys came in here and showed us their rings," he began with a laugh, "but Purzycki has a plan and he talked us through it and outlined step-by-step how he's going to have success here. He won big as a high school coach and everyone in the state knows him. He was part of a national championship at Delaware. It doesn't matter what color he is, we need a proven winner. We need to hire someone who Delawareans can identify with to get the community behind DSC football."

Hamilton had arrived at DSC a quarter century earlier and had seen just six winning football seasons.

"I'm tired of losing for 25 years," he said in a rising voice. "I want to win, and I want the program to succeed, so it doesn't matter to me what color the coach is."

When Hamilton finished Townsend chimed in, "I don't care if he's purple, or from Mars. He's the guy I want leading this program."

Dr. Mishoe had indicated all along that he would accept and give much weight to the suggestions of his athletic director and the head of the athletic council. There might have been some in the room opposed to Purzycki's hiring, but Hamilton and Townsend were clear on the direction they wanted to go. They were excused from the room and the Board of Trustees discussed their final decision.

Purzycki got home around 9:00 and spent the next half hour with his wife and his brother Mike trying to perk him up, but they could hardly argue with his conclusion that Billy Joe was obviously the school's choice.

Before long, the phone rang. It was Townsend.

"Joe, on behalf of the board of trustees and Dr. Luna Mishoe, we are offering you the head coaching job at Delaware State College."

Purzycki was shocked. Then he allowed himself to become excited and nearly overcome with emotion. He couldn't believe what he was hearing. Townsend told him a press conference was scheduled for the following morning at the school and that he should plan to arrive by 8 a.m.

"Nelson," he said, "please tell the board, you've made the right decision. I won't let you down."

Townsend hung up the phone and settled back in his office chair with more than a little satisfaction. From the minute he'd met Purzycki, he pegged him as the best guy for the job. The process had been more complicated, required an extra two weeks, had become a source of frustration and even personal embarrassment at times. But in the end, he had built a coalition of support from others who agreed with him. Purzycki's reaction to the events of the evening, his demeanor in the interview with the board of trustees, and his attention to detail clinched the deal.

The vote was 8-to-1 in favor of Purzycki with Hardcastle the only member to vote for McKinley. Billy Joe, despite his impressive resume, was not even considered in the final vote.

Townsend was exhausted, but he still had work to do. He still had to tell Billy Joe that he hadn't been hired and, in a cringe-worthy twist, he was also Joe's ride back to the Philadelphia airport. So, moments after telling him he didn't get the job, they got into Townsend's car for what must have been a fairly quiet 90-minute drive.

SIX

About 10 hours after he was offered the head coaching position at Delaware State College, Purzycki made his triumphant return to Dover for the news conference. He hadn't slept well, but he wasn't tired. His fitful sleep was due mainly to the excitement that washed over his mind as he contemplated the turn of events.

He loved football, and he wanted to be a head football coach. Yet, after he had invested more than a decade in what he hoped would become his lifelong career, he was making such a meager salary that he needed something good to happen fast. And the previous night, he'd walked through his front door convinced that the Del State job had slipped through his hands.

Would he ever get the chance to run his own program? Or would he have to consider those other options outside of football to make a living?

Then came Townsend's phone call. In that shocking instant Purzycki's dream of becoming a head coach at an NCAA Division I school had been realized and his salary more than doubled. Snow flurries and fog accompanied him on his drive, but his spirit and emotion were in such a good place that the wintry conditions barely registered with him.

He'd faced the media often as a high school head coach and he'd dealt with reporters as a player and a coach at Delaware, but this morning would be his first formal news conference. Far from intimidating him, the idea of a roomful of reporters waiting to hear his vision for building a successful program at Delaware State thrilled him.

He was dressed for the occasion, too. A few months earlier, when he was considering a career change by joining the FBI, his friend Lou Geekus had encouraged Purzycki to step up his fashion game.

"You need a new suit," Geekus advised him. "And get a haircut so you look more like a G-man than a hippy."

The FBI plan had been moved to the backburner because of Reagan's election and the accompanying budget cuts, and now that he had a new job it was taken off the stove entirely. But, in the interim, Purzycki had taken Geekus's advice and would arrive in Dover looking like a man in charge wearing new shoes, a new suit, and a new overcoat (the last item a gift from his brother).

He walked into Townsend's office a few minutes after 8:00 a.m. and for the second day in a row felt his excitement fade as Townsend greeted him with a concerned look.

"Joe, I have to talk to you before we go over to the press conference," he said gravely. "We had some problems here on campus last night."

"What are you talking about?" Purzycki responded.

"Young kids, reacting the way they sometimes do," Townsend said, searching for the right words. "Well, they kind of overdid it in the dorms. They were upset about the decision to hire you and there was a lot of anger."

The explosive reaction to Purzycki's hiring was the result of building tension on campus going back to the firing of Charles Henderson in December. Most of the players realized a coaching change was necessary, but when word got out that the school was going to invest money in the program with a new weight room, a training table, and possibly a locker room, some players were upset. They knew Henderson had asked for many of those things but never got them and that struck them as unfair.

"All of a sudden, the school was going to ante up all this money for things they could have and should have done after we went 7-and-3 in 1978," said defensive lineman Calvin Mason. "Why didn't they give the other coaches the tools they needed?"

Then came Scott Wasser's column predicting a white coach, which had not only complicated Townsend's efforts to hire Purzycki but created a lot of discussion within the team.

"The story about how you've got to hire a white coach didn't help things at all," said Mason's defensive line teammate Anthony Sharpe. "No one wanted to be told what to do and the thinking was we should get a black coach. A lot of people didn't want to change their ways."

"Most of the players were interested in bringing in a coach who was notable in the black college football space," said wide receiver Walt Samuels. "There were several heated meetings and the overriding choice of the football community and the student community was Billy Joe. He was a veteran coach and my sentiment was that he would be a better fit for us."

That opinion was the popular one among players, students, and faculty at the school. How could the school not hire Billy Joe? He checked every box the football community thought the Hornets needed in a new coach, and by the board of trustees' final interviews everyone (including Purzycki) figured Joe had the job in the bag.

The Eagles assistant himself must have felt that way as he walked over to the players' dorm to introduce himself following his interview. His hiring certainly seemed to be a fait accompli.

"Billy Joe came in and talked to us," said Samuels. "He had that pro background and he was with the Eagles and they're going to the Super Bowl. He was going to bring a pro-style offense in and we were all excited. We all thought it was a lock that he had gotten the job."

While Joe visited the players, other students milled around the library awaiting official word of his hiring. Shortly after 9 p.m., the door to the trustees' meeting room opened and chairman William Dix cleared his throat to make the announcement.

"The new head football coach at Delaware State College is," Dix began before pausing as people in the library leaned forward in anticipation, "Joe ... Purzycki." The way Dix paused as he made the announcement, combined with the fact that most people in the room thought Billy Joe was a shoo-in for the job, led to a moment of stunned silence as people realized what had happened. The guy they wanted for the job, the guy with NFL credentials and college football head coaching experience who had come to Dover from the Super Bowl just for the interview was not going to be hired.

The job instead went to the Delaware assistant. Purzycki. A guy who had no connection to the NFL, who had only been a head coach in high school, and whose only way into the Super Bowl on Sunday was if he bought a ticket.

And … he was white.

Reaction to the announcement was swift, unanimous, and loud. Students and student-athletes alike felt it was clear Billy Joe was the better and more experienced candidate and that the only possible explanation for Purzycki's hiring was that school officials had buckled under the pressure of Wasser's column.

After calling Purzycki to inform him that he had the job, Nelson hurried across campus to the player's dormitory to get Joe for the trip to the Philadelphia airport. But bad news, using its normal rate of speed, beat him there. When he walked into the dorm to find Joe the mood was already ugly.

"It was almost like a riot when they announced they were going to hire Coach Purzycki," said offensive lineman Calvin Stephens. "The students and the team all wanted Billy Joe and it was really tense in the dorm."

Tight end Terry Staples had just completed his freshman season and remembers negative reaction among some teammates based on the perceived social injustice. "A lot of players were upset. They were saying, 'How are they going to bring a white coach to a black college? We should be trying to keep black coaches employed and working.'"

Mike Colbert was a freshman hoping to walk on to the football team in 1981. "Billy Joe was a decorated NFL player who was on the staff of the Eagles, they're getting ready to go to the Super Bowl, and we find out they're gonna hire a high school coach? It was devastating."

By the time Townsend found him, Billy Joe had already heard the news. Delaware State Student Government Association president Thomas B. Moody had come directly from the library when word got out that Purzycki was the choice.

"He was disappointed when he found out he didn't get the job," Samuels remembered, "and when everyone saw how disappointed he was, we got disappointed. That's what caused the uproar."

"A lot of people thought the school had let us down," said quarterback Sam Warren. "People had become disturbed with the athletic department."

Townsend knew the players wanted Joe and he knew the players would be upset. But he was surprised at the level of anger. "I thought they would be shocked, not hostile," he said. As Townsend left the dorm with Joe for the long drive to the airport, he was the target of a pointed barb from an unknown player.

"You sold us out, Townsend! You gave it to the white people!"

That accusation had the desired effect. It stung. But Townsend knew it was pointless to engage in debate with an angry crowd, so he moved on. He also knew where he had come from. He had faced hatred, bigotry, and double-standards in his life. No one needed to lecture him about how the world worked. He believed in hiring the right person for the job no matter his skin color. And that's what he had done.

SEVEN

Elijah and Mary Townsend welcomed their first child into the world on May 16, 1941. Both just 19 years old, they lived in Horntown, Virginia, a small crossroads near the Maryland border. The area is known as Delmarva, the 170-mile-long peninsula that contains parts of Delaware, Maryland, and Virginia, bordered by the Delaware Bay and the Atlantic Ocean to the east and the Chesapeake Bay to the west.

As the United States entered World War II, Elijah worked at a lumber yard. He eventually enlisted, and after serving four years in the Navy, he spent eleven years working at the nearby Chincoteague Naval Air Station.

Mary, unlike Elijah, had graduated from high school and worked in a Birdseye frozen foods plant. She usually worked the night shift, so she could be around the house during the day with Nelson and his younger brother Rudie. They were brought up in a home where hard work was required, education was important, and Mary's word was law.

Among their chores at home was tending to the family fields, where Nelson and Rudie were expected to work until their baskets were filled to mom's satisfaction.

Nelson loved the okra dishes his mom cooked, but picking the vegetable was another matter. He recalled how the spiny texture would leave him scratched and itchy. And then there was okra's distinctive smell of cat pee. He hated everything about okra except eating it.

In school, he faced the same challenge his parents had dealt with 20 years earlier: there was still exactly one high school on all of Virginia's Eastern Shore that allowed black students. So, just as they had, Nelson spent an hour each way on a bus to attend Mary N. Smith

High School. He was a bright student who had been passed through lower grades, so he would graduate early. Still, his plans extended only through finishing high school, even though his parents had hoped he would continue his education beyond that.

It took only one day in his first real job – in the summer of 1956 – for his future to take a determined direction. That one day of working in a chicken processing plant convinced 15-year-old Nelson that picking okra wasn't the worst thing in the world, and that school was far from that. Eight hours working on a never-ending assembly line of dead chickens gives a guy plenty of time to think. And by the time he got home, Nelson knew what he thought. He entered the house, saw his mother, and made a proclamation that was music to her ears: "I am going to college."

By August of 1958, at just 17 years old, he enrolled at Maryland State College (MSC), 30 minutes north in Princess Anne, Maryland. Part of the extensive network of Historically Black Colleges and Universities formed after the Civil War, MSC gave black students from Delmarva a local place to further their education.

During college, Townsend had a summer job in a hotel in Ocean Shores, Maryland, working in a restaurant where he was not allowed to dine – one of the accepted indignities of the day. He and his fellow workers were, however, allowed to live in the basement of the hotel.

He liked the job, learned some serious cooking skills, and at Maryland State got his first taste of intercollegiate athletics. He became a three-year starter on the school's baseball team, and the accompanying travel allowed him to experience and develop pride in the fabric of HBCUs during the civil rights movement in the 1950s and '60s.

Upon graduation in 1962 Townsend got a job teaching in the Worcester County school system – the first African American teacher hired by the county, and he felt the full responsibility of his opportunity. He saw the job as a way to open doors for others and he knew that he could change preconceived notions that some might have about hiring black educators.

He spent a decade in the region as a teacher, counselor, vice-principal, as well as coaching baseball, basketball, and football at Pocomoke High School for three years.

In 1976, he was hired as vice president of student affairs at his alma mater, which by then was known as the University of Maryland Eastern Shore. When the school's athletic director quit, Townsend was selected as his replacement. Running a school's athletic department kept him involved in so many of the avocations he enjoyed, and he was good at it.

At UMES he also got to know a co-worker named Diane. They had a lot in common. They had both been married before, they both had two kids, they both worked in education, and they both liked each other. A lot. They were married in 1979, shortly before Townsend accepted the job as athletic director at Delaware State.

Now, in the winter and spring of 1981, he faced his biggest challenge since arriving in Dover: dealing with a student body and football team that was categorically not on board with the decision to hire Purzycki, while at the same time convincing Purzycki that everything was going to be fine. As he had done during the protracted search and interview process, Townsend tried to downplay to Purzycki the events of the previous night.

"They're students," he said. "They'll get over it."

Townsend and Purzycki walked over to the news conference together, and both were struck at how quiet it was on campus. It was decidedly less quiet in the auditorium, which was packed with students along with the reporters.

Purzycki sat at his seat at a rectangular table in the center of the room and felt his heartbeat quicken as he picked up on the confrontational vibe in the room and realized that maybe not everyone was ready to "get over it."

Dr. Mishoe and Townsend each spoke for a few minutes about how excited they were to have Purzycki at Delaware State. They listed his accomplishments, talked about the good times ahead for the program and then opened the floor for questions for their new coach.

But the first question was more of a statement:

"The players and the students all wanted Billy Joe to be the head coach. Students protested your hiring last night and plan to hold similar protests today. What's your reaction to that?"

The bluntness caught Purzycki off guard, but he recovered quickly. He heard himself say something about just wanting to be a football coach and to build something successful at DSC.

"Do you realize that there are a group of players who are organizing a boycott and are threatening not to play for you?"

"Mr. Townsend shared with me that some of the students were unhappy about the decision," he said. "Here's the way I'm approaching this situation: I understand there's never been a white coach at an HBCU and I understand the sensitivity of the students here to that situation. But I have one job and that's to produce a first-class football program. That's what I'm going to do."

"There's a rumor among the students and the players that you're going to turn us into the University of Delaware and recruit primarily white players for the team. Is that true?"

Purzycki admitted that he would borrow from Delaware's system and attempt to duplicate their success in Dover but that there was no plan to exclusively recruit white players.

"You're being given many benefits like a weight room, a larger staff of full-time assistants, and a locker room that were all denied to the previous coach, who was black. Do you think that is fair?"

On it went. He had prepared himself for questions about race but had not anticipated the succession of barbs and questions regarding protests and petitions, with football seemingly on the periphery.

He called the Portland State game "a terrible injustice" and promised to "get things going and get things turned around. And when we do that everyone is going to know who we are."

He explained his five-point plan for the program. He would recruit players primarily from within two hours of campus, install Delaware's Wing-T offense, use the new weight room to improve the team's strength-conditioning program, hire good assistant coaches, and build support within the community.

"My immediate goal is to improve and as long as we show marked improvement I'll be happy. I'm a realist but I also think there's no limit to what can be done. We have some good football players here and we have the support of Mr. Townsend and the college."

A reporter brought things back around to the color of Purzycki's skin and the campus-wide disapproval of his hiring.

"I don't think the race issue will be a problem for me, whatsoever," he said. "It may be with some people, but I hope I can overcome that quickly. I'm a football coach and I'd like to put everything else aside. My program is going to have consistency, fairness, and integrity throughout."

The news conference eventually ended and Purzycki stood and made small talk with some of the Delaware State administration. As he looked around the room, he realized the division that marked the news conference was continuing as reporters got reaction from some of the people gathered.

"We've got a good man," said Board of Trustees chairman William Dix. "I think he's the best one for the job."

"The vote was 8-to-1 in favor of him," added school president Luna Mishoe. "That should tell you something."

Trustee Richard Barros said the school was lucky to get Purzycki and praised the new coach for having a "structural plan, organization, and enthusiasm to build a successful program."

Even trustee James Hardcastle, who had opposed Purzycki's hiring, blocked Townsend's original expedited plan, and insisted the school talk to Jim McKinley about the job, sounded a positive note. "I nominated Mr. McKinley and I thought he was the best choice. But I support Mr. Purzycki 100 percent."

All good. But in another corner of the room student president Thomas Moody was sounding the alarm. Word had leaked that in their final meeting the trustees never considered hiring Billy Joe despite the fact he was the athletic council's top choice for the job. (Moody was a member of the athletic council.) The trustees had debated only McKinley vs. Purzycki, which rankled Moody. He promised it also wouldn't be received well by his constituents.

"Speaking for the students," he told the *Delaware State News*, "I don't think they'll be very happy. I'm displeased with the attitude of the body of representatives of this institution. I think they let politics control everyday occurrences. I feel there was a lot of pressure applied by the media to hire Purzycki due to racial overtones."

Eventually, people were done asking questions. The new coach of the Hornets was a little shaken at what he had just gone through, but he felt he had handled things OK and he got excited again as he and Townsend made their way to the day's next appointment: his first official meeting with his team.

This is a moment Purzycki had thought about for several weeks. His desire to be a leader of young men was his primary reason for taking the job and he couldn't wait to stand in front of a group of players and share with them his vision for how they were going to become successful at Delaware State. He entered the meeting room a few minutes early, spread his notes on the lectern, and thought about what he wanted to say.

Only five players showed up.

Purzycki nervously checked his watch and continually glimpsed the doorway. He eventually realized that no one else was coming. He made a few comments and thanked the players who were there.

As he gathered his unused notes and prepared to leave he was approached by defensive lineman Alfred Parham. A sophomore, Parham knew his new coach was more than a little disappointed that so many players had decided to skip the meeting. Purzycki now realized that talk of a boycott was more than just talk. But Parham counseled patience.

"Coach, you've got to understand, the fellas are just a little disturbed," he said. "It was a little shocking to all of us to find out we were going to have a white football coach."

Life indeed comes down to a few moments and how you choose to handle them. Purzycki's mind was a roiling sea of shock, anger, and sadness. This day was supposed to be one of the best of his life, maybe *the* best from a professional standpoint. But the news conference had devolved from an expected moment of triumph to a series of questions that left him understandably defensive. His first team meeting was both a disaster and an embarrassment and as he stood in the nearly empty meeting room trying to avoid either screaming in rage or crying out in anguish, here was this 20-year-old kid telling him how things were. Purzycki briefly searched for a proper response when Townsend's words from a month earlier came back to him.

"Your biggest problem is this: you're going to find out what it's like to be in the minority. It's YOU who's going to have to see everybody else's side of things. And I can tell you right now it's not going to be easy."

Purzycki took a deep breath and collected his thoughts. He looked Parham in the eye and saw a young man who was sincere in his desire to ease Purzycki's anxiousness. Parham had attended the meeting, one of only five who did, and was the first player reaching out to engage the new coach. He deserved the courtesy of a sincere reply.

"Alfred, all I want to convey to everybody – and I hear all the things the press is saying – is that I'm not here to change anything. I'm not here as an agent of the University of Delaware. I just want to build a successful football program at Delaware State College. Please, tell your teammates that."

The paltry attendance at the meeting sent a clear message that the new coach's most monumental task would be to win over his own team.

"A lot of players were still shocked," said Terry Staples. "They were like, 'Oh, no. Not a white coach here. Nope, nope, nope, nope.'"

"There were a lot of guys in the dorm saying, 'I'm not going to that meeting because he's not going to be MY head coach," said Mike Colbert. There was also some confusion about the meeting.

"There were definitely people who didn't go," said Anthony Sharpe. "But a lot of guys didn't know or didn't realize that we were supposed to go. I don't remember it being said that it was mandatory that we attend, and I think some guys missed it because of bad communication."

Matt Horace agrees with Sharpe that there was a communication breakdown but emphasized that the idea of a boycott of the new coach among the players was a very real thing.

"The temperament among many players was that they weren't going to play for a white coach at an HBCU. It was very real. There were petitions going around and there were several players who were very adamant that they were not going to play for Purzycki. All of that was driven in a large part by the culture of the school, and the HBCU community."

Part of the culture at DSC was to be suspicious of anything that involved the University of Delaware owing in part to an incident three decades earlier. After World War II, enrollment at Del State had increased dramatically due to the G.I. Bill (a government program created to help veterans get a college education). But the school didn't have the budget or facilities necessary to handle the rising student body. DSC thus lost its accreditation and by 1951 was struggling to stay open.

One idea in the legislature was to somehow merge the two schools in an effort to save DSC. In a letter to Governor Elbert N. Carvel, UD officials not only rejected that plan but recommended that Delaware State College simply be shuttered.

Some of the faculty members and administrators at DSC in 1981 had been on the staff (or were students) when that letter was sent, and they were still angry at the thought that when DSC was struggling, those at UD not only didn't provide assistance, their only idea was to close the only college in the state that served African Americans.

Since Purzycki's hiring had been rumored for a few weeks, there was plenty of time and opportunity for that story to be used by people to foment unrest at the notion of a white coach from Delaware being named as head coach at DSC.

EIGHT

Townsend suggested they get Purzycki settled into his new office. As they made their way across campus, they couldn't help but notice hundreds of students streaming to what was referred to in the *Hornet*, the student newspaper at Delaware State, as an "emergency convocation to discuss the issue of whether new head football coach Joe Purzycki was, in fact, the best qualified for the job."

The student paper left no doubt as to what they thought about Purzycki's qualifications, derisively nicknaming him "The Polish Prince."

"Someone told us that there were already 400 kids at the student center who were staging a sit-in protest," Purzycki said. "Players and students were going to speak at the protest. There were placards on the walls of buildings and we saw several students carrying protest signs."

The scene in the student center was passionate bordering on chaos.

"I remember Mr. Hamilton trying to calm everyone down," Walt Samuels said. Both times Hamilton tried to speak and explain the decision, he was shouted down by angry students.

"I had to go in front of the students and explain why we hired him," Hamilton said. They literally booed me off the stage. Players wouldn't talk to me."

Moody then got up to speak and stirred things up by declaring that despite the fact the athletic council had recommended Billy Joe as their top choice, Joe was never even considered by the trustees in their final decision.

At least two football players spoke. Freshman wide receiver Bobby Swoope told the crowd that, "a Historic Black College should have hired a black coach." He pointed to the few opportunities for black

43

head coaches in college football and that the DSC decision was making things even worse.

Calvin Mason had been vocal in challenging the school's leaders since Wasser's column had appeared two weeks earlier. Mason's primary complaint was that Purzycki was being given resources that had not been made available to the previous staff.

"I was very active in student government, so I spoke up about a lot of things around campus," he said. "I was one of the instigators of the protest. It was nothing against Purzycki. My question was why couldn't you get this stuff for the guy before him and let him build a program? I got up at a podium and spoke my mind about how I thought this whole thing was wrong."

According to a story in the *Hornet*, there was discussion among students in between speeches that Purzycki's hiring was obviously the first step in bringing more white athletes and more white students to Dover thus eroding DSC's HBCU culture.

"All of us are talking about the fact of having a white coach," a student yelled. "But what will we do about it?"

As the protest broke up, Moody led a small delegation of students and team members to the administration building where they asked to see Luna Mishoe. Once inside the president's office, the protest lost a little steam. Mishoe listened to the concerns but kept reiterating that the trustees had been impressed by Purzycki's interview and his plan for how to build long-term success at Delaware State. He reminded the players that they would benefit from the increased resources being allocated for the program. He reminded them that by increasing scholarships they were also increasing the amount of talent available to the team.

While some of the students were still dug in, many of the players listened to Mishoe and realized that the university investing in the program, no matter the timing (and no matter the head coach), was going to benefit them all.

"This is our decision," Dr. Mishoe told the group. "We're not looking at hiring someone else. We've hired Coach Purzycki and he's the guy who's going to lead our football program."

Meanwhile, Townsend and Purzycki made their way into the athletic offices. When he reached his new office at the end of the hallway, Purzycki looked around. Any hope that his day was going to turn around evaporated.

"It was a very small office," he said. "There was an empty anteroom in front of it. There was a green chalkboard with a giant hole in the middle that someone had tried to repair with plaster. There was a filing cabinet with several drill holes in one side. It looked like someone had lost the keys at one point and then used a drill on it, so they could get in."

Purzycki sat down at his desk and took it all in. He realized it was cold in the room and looked for a thermostat to adjust the heat. It was then that he noticed one of the windows was broken leaving the room open to the icy January breeze. The wastebasket was full. An ashtray spilled over. Purzycki looked at his desk phone and sighed.

"The receiver was hanging from the phone by the wires and athletic tape. It was caked with a yellow substance that looked like dried eggs. It was filthy."

He picked the phone up and was shocked to find out that it worked. His first official act as head coach at Delaware State was to use that phone to call the phone company to order a new phone. Purzycki hung up and sat at the desk. At Delaware, even the defensive backs coach had a first-rate office. Now, as he sat in his overcoat in a room with no heat, looking at a phone held together by athletic tape, a broken file cabinet, and a chalkboard with a hole in it, and as he considered everything else he had been through, Purzycki had a chilling thought.

"Tubby was right," he said to himself. "What have I done? I left Camelot for this?"

Purzycki left the office and found Townsend. He had a few routine HR documents to fill out and he needed Townsend to show him where he had to go to get that done.

As they walked Purzycki's mind raced: "I was so exhausted. I didn't expect 400 protestors. I didn't expect the players not to show up for the meeting. I didn't expect the office to look as pathetic and rundown as it was. I never expected the tidal wave that I walked into. I felt sick to my stomach. It was the loneliest day of my life. I began to think this might be a huge mistake in judgment on my part."

Finally, he stopped walking and turned to face his new boss. "Nelson, I just don't know if this is going to work."

Townsend looked at Purzycki in silence. He knew the day hadn't unfolded in any way Purzycki could have possibly envisioned. But he liked how he had handled the news conference and was especially happy with how he had spoken to Parham after the aborted team meeting. He thought DSC had the right man for the job. So, he was taken aback to hear Purzycki gathering the white flag.

"I *told* you that you were going to have to be tough and that this *wasn't going to be easy*," Townsend said his voice rising in anger. "We're *not* having a bunch of 18 and 19-year-olds tell us what to do. This is going to pass, Joe. We have bigger things to do here."

Townsend's anger had a clarifying effect on Purzycki who suddenly realized the full extent of what his new boss had put himself through to give him the chance he'd wanted. Townsend had been getting hit from all sides since Wasser's column had been published.

For two weeks the AD had been confronted by students, players, faculty, staff, and alumni, all wanting to know just what in the hell he was thinking promoting a white man as the new head coach at Del State (and a white man from Delaware, to boot). Townsend was irritated with the tone of the questions at the news conference and he was furious that so many members of the team elected to skip the first meeting with their new head coach. He was angry, but he was not going to allow Purzycki to even consider walking away now.

"We have bigger things to do here," he repeated. "I don't want to hear anything about this again."

Purzycki knew, from that moment, he was not alone. He and Townsend were in the fight together.

"If Nelson had shown even the slightest bit of hesitancy," Purzycki recalled years later, "if he had given any indication that he agreed with me that it might not work, I would have driven home and asked Tubby for my job back at Delaware.

"Instead, I knew I had his full support and I wasn't going to back out because he needed me as much as I needed him. Quitting at that point would have been the wrong thing to do. He was dependent on me and I knew he was in my corner."

The moment passed, and he was anxious to get home.

He knew Sharon was in his corner, too, and needed her perspective. On his drive, he replayed the events of the day while doubt again clouded his mind.

"What have I gotten myself into?" Purzycki said as he walked his wife through his Kafkaesque first day on the job. He detailed the press conference, the meeting, the protest, and the condition of his office. She waited for him to finish.

"I've got some good news for you," she offered. "You've had a dozen phone calls from friends today and they've all said the same thing. They all said this is the greatest thing and they all think you're going to turn the place around."

She showed him the list of callers and Purzycki felt a lump rising in his throat. Players he had coached in high school and at Delaware. Guys he had coached with and guys he had coached against. Friends from his days growing up in New Jersey. Every message had a common theme.

"You are the man for this job. You will get things going in the football program at Delaware State College."

There are rare moments in a person's life when the past comes into focus as part of the present. That those prior experiences indeed have impacted people in ways we might not have realized at the time. This was such a moment for Joe Purzycki.

"I looked at the list and started thinking that a lot of people I love and respect think this is a special opportunity where I could really have a positive impact and do good work," he said.

Purzycki called a few people back to thank them and began to focus on the positive aspects of his new job. He had a team to lead and if the players who were there didn't want to play for him, he would find guys who would. He had an idea of who he wanted on his staff and he could begin seriously working on that plan. Delaware State had more than doubled his salary and that was no small thing. They could afford a second car now bringing an end to the days of coordinating schedules with his wife around just one. They could find a house in Dover for their growing family. He and Sharon began discussing everything and she reminded him that 24 hours earlier he was crushed because he thought he *didn't* get the job. Now, he had the job. It was time to think about the positives.

"We were so young," Sharon said. "We didn't think about it not working. We were optimistic it would work. We had lived in Dover (in Purzycki's days as a high school coach) and we had great friends in Dover, so it was like going home. In the back of my mind, I knew all along he was going to get it. I just knew. I never doubted it. And he had such a great relationship with his new boss. He really loved and trusted Nelson from the start."

Purzycki's spirits were further buoyed when the phone rang, and Townsend was on the other end of the line. But the message the AD delivered boomeranged the day back into darkness.

"Listen, Joe, I just got a call from the Delaware State Police. A woman called the Dover newspaper and made a death threat against you. Now, I don't want you to worry because this is just a crank. She wouldn't even leave her name."

Purzycki was stunned. He told Sharon what Nelson had just told him.

"Well, I didn't want to worry you," his wife said. "but a man called here earlier and said something about how you'd better not ever set foot on campus again. I didn't take him seriously, but he was loud and angry."

Purzycki relayed that to Townsend.

"OK," Townsend said, "it's a couple of cranks. It's nothing. They wouldn't even identify themselves. The state police are telling me the same thing, but they want to err on the side of caution, so they think you should not come to work tomorrow, and we can wait until Monday to get started."

Purzycki took a deep breath and agreed with his boss and his wife. There was nothing to this nonsense and it wasn't worth worrying about. Nevertheless, after watching hundreds of people protest he knew there was some real anger on campus. He agreed to take Friday off and he promised Townsend he would see him first thing Monday morning.

He spent the rest of the evening reflecting on the events of the past few days. He knew his hiring would stir up some emotions at Delaware State, but he was surprised at how deep some people's feelings ran. He thought about how odd it felt to be judged solely by the color of his skin.

It would be a vast overstatement to say he now knew what it was like to be black in America. But in one day he had gotten a pretty good peek into that window and it left him contemplating his life's journey to this point.

He had long ago come to believe that black people and white people were the same. There were some cultural differences (food, music, fashion, etc.) but in the end, they wanted the same basic things out of life. And he was counting on some of that understanding to help him recruit players with their parents accepting that he was on their side.

Now he was beginning to realize that there was a lot more to it than that. He couldn't feel the emotions the upset students and players were experiencing, but he could recognize that they had good reasons for feeling that way.

NINE

Joe Purzycki was never a big kid growing up in Newark, New Jersey, and when he was seven, he had a tough break that put him further behind the kids in his neighborhood.

Born on February 20, 1947, the second of two boys to Mike and Marie, he took to sports well, much like his dad and big brother Mike. But unlike them, size became an issue early for Joe.

Purzycki missed all of second grade because of a bad bout of pneumonia and scarlet fever. "When my mom brought me back to Sacred Heart school in January the nuns said to keep me home because I was so emaciated. My brother was big and strong, but I was always small and undersized, particularly after the illness."

Small kids tended to get picked on, but he had someone keeping an eye out for him. "On the tough streets of Newark, my big brother became my guardian," he said, "and my lifelong best friend. My dad, who everyone called 'Iron Mike,' made it clear to my brother that he was expected to look after me."

As a result, Joe frequently wound up playing with bigger kids, which helped him to never become overwhelmed when facing full-sized opponents in high school and college. He also compensated with his understanding of sports and his unusually strong will.

Growing up, the Purzyckis lived in a small apartment in Ivy Hill, a series of several 15-story red brick rectangular buildings in Upper Vailsburg. Their dad had been a star athlete at Southside High in Newark and played football and basketball at Villanova. He served in World War II, eventually became a car salesman in downtown Newark and was well known around the city.

When the Purzycki boys weren't playing sports, they were often at their grandparents' house. Antony and Stella Purzycki emigrated from Warsaw, Poland, as teenagers and settled in a Polish enclave in Newark. The Purzycki boys nicknamed them "Babci and Lala." Babci is Polish for grandmother. Their grandfather would sing to young Mike and Joe to entertain them but couldn't speak English so instead of the words to a song he would just sing "La la la la." So, they called him Lala.

Lala and Babci had six kids so there were always people around the house. "Our aunts and uncles poured affection over us and were interested in our lives," Purzycki said.

The new Americans struggled with their new language and never quite adapted to other aspects of American culture. They often felt discrimination when dealing with people from outside the neighborhood, who called them dumb and lazy for not knowing English. It hurt Purzycki to see this happen. He knew his grandparents were wise and it didn't bother him that they weren't always able to speak with him.

"There was not much in terms of material goods, but the house was full of love," Purzycki said. "And even though neither of them spoke much English, we were able to share our love for one another with very little verbal communication."

Purzycki's mom Marie also came from a big family. Marie was the youngest of three daughters born to Joe Pascal and Mae Carlin. When she was four, her mother died, leaving her dad alone with the task of raising three girls.

Eventually, her father remarried, and his second wife (Ella) brought two sons to the new family. Those five children eventually had a dozen kids of their own so Purzycki grew up around plenty of cousins (including six on his dad's side of the family).

Joe Pascal was a politician, an impressive orator, and an impeccable dresser. In his later years (after Ella died) he moved in with his youngest daughter's family. "There were always politicians visiting us and there were always interesting discussions going on around the dining room table," Purzycki said. "My family on both sides were all blue-collar people. Family dinners, birthdays, confirmations, and weddings were all very important. We were incredibly close."

In 1959 the family moved from their small apartment to a nearby house in lower Vailsburg. As Purzycki entered his teen years he had developed into a three-sport athlete and, despite his size, he was particularly good at football.

Joe weighed all of 105 pounds when he went out for the freshman football team at Vailsburg. Mike, two years older and 85 pounds heavier, showed his little brother how to slip some ankle weights into his jersey when he showed up to weigh in for tryouts to make himself a little bigger.

By the time Joe was a junior he had put on a little more weight, but his protector was off to the University of Delaware, beginning a record-setting career as a receiver.

The Purzyckis let their boys choose where they wanted to go to high school. Although his brother elected to attend Seton Hall Prep, an athletic powerhouse where most of his friends were, Joe and his buddies went to Vailsburg High in their neighborhood. This was good for staying close to his best friends but bad for football. There were seven city high schools in Newark; Vailsburg had the worst football team of them all.

His junior season, the Vikings won just one game and Purzycki began to consider transferring for his senior season. He was emerging as a good player, his brother had gotten a scholarship to Delaware, and he and his dad both felt he needed to be at a school with more football visibility if that was going to happen for Joe.

The lousy season was overshadowed in retrospect by something more important. His junior year was the first time Purzycki had played with African American teammates. In an effort to avoid court-ordered busing to desegregate schools, the city of Newark school system in 1964 allowed students to choose where they wanted to go. Several African American students began attending classes that fall at Vailsburg High.

For the first time, Purzycki began to study, socialize, and compete with black kids. He found out that they were just kids, too. Gradually at first, he started to question the veracity of the portrayal of African Americans that he'd heard his entire life.

"I had grown up in an ethnic family in an all-white neighborhood. There was always a characterization or portrayal of African Americans that was very unflattering. When you're young and you don't have any other experience, you think 'I guess that's just how things are' and you begin to adopt those feelings."

That notion was being challenged. Going to school with black classmates and competing with black athletes showed him what was real, rather than what he'd been led to believe. That journey is a personal one and some chose not to take it. For Purzycki, Donald Bernard became a significant person in opening his eyes to greater awareness. They met at basketball tryouts, and they quickly became friends.

"Becoming friends with Donny was the first big awakening for me," he said. "There were other black kids who I met and played sports with and I started to change and began seeing these guys in a different light. There were two basketball courts behind Vailsburg High that were used nightly during the summer for pickup games. There were kids from all over the city at these games. Kids of all races and ethnicities. You'd get to know guys while waiting on the sidelines for the next game and all of those encounters reinforced my emerging belief that these guys weren't very different from me."

Not everyone at his school shared that thought. In the spring of his junior year, Purzycki convinced Bernard to run for a student government position at Vailsburg. Purzycki had been active in that area but was planning on transferring, so he helped Bernard launch a campaign. Eventually, Purzycki was approached by a couple students who indicated that Bernard should be discouraged from running because he was black.

Purzycki's emerging realization that skin color was no reason to judge anyone led to him dismissing the suggestion that Bernard shouldn't run. His feelings that his friend would be good for student government weren't unique. Bernard was elected with a whopping 80% of the vote.

His transfer to Our Lady of the Valley in Orange for his senior year paid off. The team was unbeaten, won the state title, and Purzycki was named to the all-state team. Since he was still undersized, he and his dad agreed it would be best for him to spend a year in prep school at Bordentown Military Institute. There, Purzycki continued to play football, got a little bigger, and was recruited as a defensive back by Vanderbilt, Boston College, William and Mary, Tennessee, and

Delaware. He wanted to go to William and Mary, but his dad sold his youngest son on another idea.

"Mike is going to be a senior at Delaware this year and I'd like to be able to see both my sons at one place," his dad told him. He didn't say it, but his father also still worried about his youngest son and wanted him to be back with his brother who could look out for him as he entered college life. Family had always been important to Purzycki and he saw the wisdom in his dad's request. Besides…

"In our house what Iron Mike said was always the final word," Purzycki laughed. "So, I was going to Delaware to play football for the Blue Hens."

His freshman year at UD was typical of the life of a first-year college student. He adjusted to being on his own (albeit with help from his brother) and learned how to manage his time. Freshman football kept him busy in the fall.

By the spring of 1967, he had made many new friends at Delaware and he often spent time with them discussing the series of divisive social issues playing out in America that affected everyone and left many, including Purzycki, torn.

He was against the Vietnam war. That was an unusual stance for an athlete to take at the time and it would put him at odds with his father and his uncles when he got home for the summer. They had fought in World War II. They had fought in Korea. They didn't want to hear a lot of anti-war nonsense.

He was troubled by some of what he heard at student events he attended on campus. Delaware, like many campuses at the time, was home to an increasingly radicalized student population. Students spoke out about the war, social injustice, and civil rights.

Purzycki was a proponent of the civil rights movement, but it troubled him that the tone of some of the activists who gave speeches that spring made him feel it was time for everyone to choose sides. "I didn't like feeling that I was the enemy," he said. "That was uncomfortable."

As the school year ended and he returned to New Jersey he found himself conflicted about many things, which made him a typical young person at the time, as spring rolled into what would become known as the "long, hot, summer of '67."

TEN

JULY 14, 1967

O n a pleasant Friday night in the Vailsburg neighborhood of Newark, New Jersey, Albert Avena's going away party was in full roar.

Avena had been drafted and was due to report to the Army. The conflict in Southeast Asia was starting to look more like a war than a "police action" (the benign term the U. S. government was still using) and more young men were being called into service. For most of them, Vietnam was the likely destination.

Any reason is reason enough to have a party in the glorious years between youth and adulthood, and Avena's departure certainly fit the bill. Neighborhood tradition held that when a guy was drafted, his buddies would throw him a huge send-off with kegs of beer and a band.

Vailsburg had two sections, Upper Vailsburg and Lower Vailsburg which were loosely divided by Sanford Avenue. The population was largely made up of Italian and Irish Catholics so the locus of Vailsburg was Sacred Heart Church which sat where Sanford Avenue intersected South Orange Avenue. The church played a large role in everything that happened in the community and the fact that it was on a hill made it seem even more imposing and immense than it was.

The neighborhood was blue-collar and home primarily to cops, firefighters, teachers, and factory workers. The shared cultural backgrounds and similar economic status that prevailed throughout Vailsburg made it a tight-knit community.

Much of the planning for the party had taken place at Sturges candy store which was just a few blocks from Sacred Heart on Cliff Street. Purzycki was at the center of those plans.

Sturges sold ice cream, candy, and sodas but its primary use for Purzycki and his friends was as a meeting place and corner hangout. "Every day we'd meet up there," he said. "It would start out with a few guys, then the crowd would grow, and before long there would be 20 to 25 guys. We'd be busting each other's balls, arranging a football, basketball, or stick-ball game depending on the season, and planning what we were going to do on the weekend."

That weekend the plan revolved around Avena's going away party. Purzycki's friend Dave Fargnoli had talked to his father Silvio about getting a hall. Silvio Fargnoli was a member of a social club called the East Orange Civic Club where many of the Italian-American men in the neighborhood would gather to share news, drink, and play bocce (it was somewhat like a later-in-life version of Sturges). He arranged for his son and his friends to use the group's party hall.

At the party they talked, laughed, drank beer, and danced to a cover band. During breaks, the hat was passed, and people tossed in a few bucks so that Avena would have some spending money for his journey. He was the man of the hour and received an unending line of hugs, backslaps, and handshakes.

But the river of beer being consumed began to expose some of the raw emotions related to the stark reality the event signified. Kids in Newark (and everywhere else) were beginning to understand that there was a thin line between a "going away" party and a "goodbye" party. Too many of their friends weren't making it back home and by the summer of 1967 young people were questioning just what in the hell we were doing in Vietnam.

They asked those questions at rallies and sit-ins. The war was the subject of dinnertime conversations at home that often quickly escalated into foot-stomping, door-slamming arguments that split cleanly along generational lines. Sometimes young people argued among themselves with anti-war sentiment squaring off against patriotism.

And bidding goodbye to a neighborhood friend who was off to an uncertain future wasn't the only thing that created nervous tension during the festive evening.

Two days earlier, Newark had become the latest of what would be 76 cities in the United States to be hit with rioting that divided cities along racial lines. More than a century after the Civil War many black Americans didn't feel the freedom they supposedly had. They watched as civil rights advocates faced violent and sometimes even fatal opposition. They knew that in their neighborhoods, jobs were scarcer and paid less. Schools were neglected and underfunded. Politicians were corrupt.

They had heard the words of activists like the late Malcolm X who said there was no such thing as a non-violent revolution. They heard Stokely Carmichael say that the black community had been non-violent for too long.

The poverty and hopelessness exploded that sweltering summer, city by city. In Newark, trouble began on the afternoon of July 12th when a peaceful protest was planned in front of the Fourth Precinct Headquarters of the police department. As protesters gathered, rumors circulated that on the previous evening the police had beaten a black cab driver after a routine traffic stop.

The crowd became agitated and by nightfall reports of violence, looting, and arrests circulated throughout the city. The following day there were sporadic outbursts of rioting with the unrest confined mainly to Newark's central ward.

By sundown Friday the local authorities were losing control of the situation and rumors began to spread throughout the city that the rioting was escalating to the point that it would include more neighborhoods.

There was a little discussion at Avena's party of the growing unrest in the city, but David Fargnoli says the idea of the conflict coming to Vailsburg seemed far-fetched.

"We knew it was happening, but it seemed far away from us. We did not think it was going to affect us."

Around 10:45, a few of the guys who had left the party early came running back into the hall and began shouting and signaling for the band to stop playing.

"Guys, guys, guys!" one of them yelled once the band had stopped. "The niggers are rioting again and now they're driving up South Orange Avenue. They're throwing Molotov cocktails at buildings in the neighborhood and they're headed this way!"

Purzycki thought back to the speakers he heard at UD who pounded the theme that the time had come to choose sides. "The country was so divided by so many things," he said. "I wondered if they were right."

It had been two months since his freshman year ended and he spent most of that time with the guys from his neighborhood. "It was an all-white environment and not everyone had an open mind about race. I still had family and friends telling me I was wrong in my belief that white people and black people weren't radically different. There were a lot of labels and prejudice that existed, and you had to acknowledge in your mind that it was there."

He was aware of what was happening in America and had seen news reports about rioting in Atlanta, Cincinnati, Buffalo, and Tampa. Now, if his friends were to be believed, similar violence was about to reach Vailsburg.

"We had all heard rumors from downtown," Purzycki said. "Three firemen were dead. A policeman had been shot. Our neighborhood was full of firemen and policemen and our feeling was if the riot was coming this way it was us against them."

"We felt like we were protecting our neighborhood," said Fargnoli. "There was a lot of chaos and it was tense. We didn't want destruction to happen in Vailsburg."

Purzycki and a dozen others piled into four cars for a quick drive over to a Dairy Queen on South Orange Avenue where they met up with several other agitated young men. At the party, they were still removed from the chaos. Now, they were less than two miles from downtown and it felt as if the riot had reached their doorstep.

"All I remember when we first got out of the cars was the overpowering acrid smell of smoke from the fires," said Purzycki.

"There was smoke and fire in the sky," Fargnoli said. "I remember you could clearly hear gunshots from downtown. Lots of gunshots. The sound of sirens was non-stop. You could hear them from all over town."

"We were teenagers," Purzycki said. "We didn't know what in the hell we were doing. I remember a lot of older folks were out of their houses and on the street."

By the time Purzycki and his friends arrived the street was lined with dozens of people. Thankfully, it was a time when handguns were still rare, so most of the people who wanted to defend their neighborhood were unarmed. The weapon of choice was supplied by numerous watering holes in the area.

"There were several Irish bars on South Orange Avenue," Purzycki said, "and the bartenders started running out to us these big beer crates made from wood and wire. Back then, quart bottles were a popular way to buy and drink beer. The crates had several big, thick brown bottles of Pabst Blue Ribbon."

Purzycki said there was no ambiguity in the message the bartenders gave to the young warriors. They were to use the beer bottles to repel any rioters attempting to enter the neighborhood.

As common sense continued to wane the group concocted the theory that the rioters were coming to destroy Sacred Heart Catholic Church. So now religious fervor was mixed into the toxic stew that the evening had become.

"All of a sudden," Purzycki recalled, "a green truck came roaring up the street with three guys in the front and two guys in the bed behind the cab. People were waving at us and yelling 'Here they come!'"

Purzycki and his friends began unloading 40-ounce beer missiles at the truck. Ironically, the amount of beer they had consumed that evening impacted their aim and damage to the green truck was minimal.

"The guys in the truck were smart enough to have their windows open so we couldn't break them, the guys in the back ducked down so we didn't hit any of them, and the truck was moving fast."

Fargnoli had just bought a new car that he was using to commute to college at Seton Hall. "It was a 1965 yellow Chevy Malibu," he said, "and one of the guys there got the bright idea to grab the jack out of the trunk of the car."

"Someone threw it and it felt like everything was in slow motion," Purzycki said. "I remember seeing the jack helicopter through the air before it smashed into the truck."

The impact of the jack got the driver's attention. The truck skidded to a stop, turned around, and began a quick retreat (through another hailstorm of beer bottles) back towards downtown. Purzycki and his pals jumped up and down and excitedly congratulated each other for defending their neighborhood. No one in the group noticed that everyone else on the corner had already gone back into the bars.

Suddenly two police cars roared up to the street corner with sirens on and lights flashing. The police quickly jumped out and confronted the group.

"That's it!" one of them yelled. "Everybody out of here! You kids go home! We've got a curfew, and everybody's gotta be off the street.'"

Usually, they all would have obeyed a direct order from a cop. But the wild surge of adrenaline after the brief conflict led to a collective willingness to question authority. Among those yelling the loudest was a big, athletic kid named Billy Conover.

"What the hell are you harassing us for?" Conover said. "Go get the guys who are shooting firemen and cops."

A police officer walked up to Conover and hit him on the side of the head. Conover was staggered for an instant and the officer grabbed him and threw him in the back seat of the police car before quickly turning around to address his stunned friends.

"Everybody is OFF this corner for curfew. If I come back and you're still here, you're going to jail. You guys pull any more shit tonight and I'm going to arrest you. Do you understand me?"

The swift show of force completely changed the mood and the group of would-be neighborhood defenders meekly retreated to their cars to go home. Purzycki was struck by how quiet it had gotten in the area. Minutes earlier the corner had been full of angry people. Now, nothing.

"That entire night is indelibly set in my mind."

"It was jarring to us," said Fargnoli. "We never considered our neighborhood dangerous. After that night, we were more careful when we went out because we thought it wasn't safe. It wasn't our little world on the corner anymore."

Rioting continued for a few more days in Newark and historians agree that the decision by the state to deploy almost 8,000 police officers and members of the National Guard only escalated tension and led to more problems.

"There was a real fear in the city," said Purzycki. "There was a fear to drive. There were so many snipers in the city. I remember going over to my girlfriend's house, and I'm slouched down low in the seat and looking both ways. You couldn't get off the highway without showing ID to show you lived there, and they weren't letting anyone in or out of downtown. It was a terrifying time."

"See," many of Purzycki's neighbors and friends said in condescending tones. "See how THEY are?"

But for Purzycki, the rioting and his brief participation in it served as a dividing line for his personal belief. People at UD were saying it was time to choose a side. Now, Purzycki had first-hand experience of what choosing sides can lead to: an atmosphere of hate and tension that literally tore the city apart.

In all, 26 people were killed in the Newark riots, 100 more were injured. Several hundred people were arrested, and over $10 million dollars in property damage was done. All of it caused by people choosing a side over something Purzycki had come to believe should have been irrelevant: the color of someone's skin.

It was time to make a choice, all right. The choice Purzycki made was to redouble his efforts to be open-minded and to further educate himself by talking and listening to people about what was causing this divide and what could be done to close it.

He had limited success with some of his relatives. The neighborhood was made up primarily of people of Polish, Irish, and Italian descent who had all faced prejudice when they had arrived in America.

"Look at Lala and Babci," they said. "They had problems when they came to America, but they pulled themselves up by their bootstraps and overcame it."

Purzycki couldn't help but compare that sentiment to Dr. Martin Luther King's quote, "It is a cruel jest to tell a bootless man to lift himself by his own bootstraps."

"You can't compare the two," he said. "Don't even try because it's not even in the realm of comparisons. Black people were enslaved and brought here against their will. They weren't allowed to read and write. For hundreds of years, it was against the law to educate them. They were lynched. The pull yourselves up by the bootstraps deal is a flawed argument. It doesn't hold any water at all."

In discussions with friends, he pointed out that by insulating themselves within the neighborhood they prevented themselves from being open to change.

"You don't understand," he'd tell them. "Black people are no different from us. There are cultural and economic differences, but you've got all this prejudice because you don't know one black guy. You don't have one close relationship with a black person."

He believed that bigotry and hate were learned behaviors ("Young kids aren't born hating people, they are taught to hate people.") and he wasn't buying into it. Friends and relatives listened with varying degrees of acceptance. A few saw his point, but most were dug in and resisted any effort to change. But there was one big person Purzycki was able to reach.

"I felt like I was able to make some progress with my dad regarding his views on race," he said. "He got to know some of my teammates and it opened his eyes."

Purzycki told his father about guys like Ronnie Whittington, Sonny and Conway Hayman, and Ted Gregory. He was particularly close to Gregory (they played together, coached together, and eventually got their master's degrees together) and their friendship included substantial discussions.

"We had a great relationship and could talk openly about things. Ted helped me understand things better. He'd give me his perspective on things and that gave me better insight into what was playing out in front of me."

His brother was like-minded and after time spent listening to his sons and meeting their friends, Iron Mike was getting it.

"He started to see what we were seeing, that these were good guys who were just like us. We were just a bunch of college kids trying to figure out how the world worked. We had the same hopes, dreams, and aspirations even though we came from different cultures."

ELEVEN

Purzycki's football career at UD concluded with an avalanche of excellence. His junior year the Blue Hens went 8-and-3. He was appointed team captain his senior season, led the country with nine interceptions, and was named an All-American. The team went 9-and-2 and for the second year won the Boardwalk Bowl in Atlantic City.

He continued to be aware of and educate himself on the emerging social upheaval taking place at Delaware and other colleges around the country. His senior year, he participated in an evening candlelight vigil against the war in Vietnam. The protest was organized by the Students for a Democratic Society (SDS), a political movement active on many campuses which, among other causes, was decidedly anti-war. The protesters at UD were surprised to see the captain of the football team standing with them.

"For a jock to do that was quite counter to what was going on in those days," Purzycki said. "The ROTC guys, the frat guys, and the sports guys usually stayed with the norm. They thought the SDS guys were flag-burning rebels who were against everything they stood for. And the guys with SDS thought I was the image of the side of things they were against. They hated me and couldn't believe an athlete might share the same beliefs they did."

Purzycki had a run-in with several of the SDS folks at an earlier protest when they did attempt to burn an American flag. He believed it was possible to be anti-war and still be pro-America and thought burning the flag was wrong. He spoke up about it and confronted the flag-burners which is what led to the SDS finding it hard to believe he had any real interest in participating in their event.

But Purzycki had educated himself on Vietnam and had seen enough young people make one-way trips there to be sure about his feelings. He felt that what students were opposing in Vietnam, and what African Americans were opposing in America were rooted in similar ground. They had finally reached the point that they refused to accept these things simply because that's the way things had always been. These things were wrong and needed to be challenged.

Purzycki could feel the changes happening in society and in himself. "I had grown up in an atmosphere of intolerance, and had gone through the riots," he said, "and I could understand that something was really wrong here. It all really impacted me."

Upon graduation, he tried to make a go of it in a semi-pro league with the legendary Pottstown Firebirds of the Atlantic Coast Football League but was injured early in his first season. Purzycki was finally ready to stop playing football and move on with his life.

His coach at Delaware, Tubby Raymond, had convinced New Jersey coaching legend Ralph Borges at Kearny High School to hire Purzycki as an assistant coach for the 1971 season. The boss of the Blue Hens promised Purzycki he would eventually find a job for him as a head coach at a high school in Delaware.

That happened the very next year when Purzycki was hired at Woodbridge High School. It was one of the smallest schools in the state, located in a rural area near Bridgeville, Delaware. The entire scene was foreign to Purzycki and his new bride, Sharon, who had been hired to teach at the elementary school in town.

"We drove down there for the first time at night, and I remember we saw all these buildings off the road with lights on," Purzycki said. "I asked Sharon if she'd ever seen so many motels in her life."

The Purzyckis had taken jobs in the heart of poultry country. What they thought were motels were actually huge chicken coops. There was a processing plant just across the state line in Maryland and most kids in the school were from families that were somehow involved in the poultry farming business.

"It was one of the poorest areas in the state," Purzycki said. "A lot of the kids had to work before they came to school to help their families. They'd spend from the time they woke up until when they came to school taking care of chickens, feeding them, cleaning out their coops. There were several jobs to be done and none of them were good. Many of the kids would come to school exhausted and smelling of chicken manure. Some of them lived in a place called Coverdale Crossroads that had no running water. I had seen poverty in the city. But I'd never seen it in the country, and it was eye-opening."

Like many small towns, Bridgeville was segregated with white and black neighborhoods. Purzycki noticed that his team reflected that divide: the black guys would sit on one side of the meeting room and the white guys on the other. It was the same in the cafeteria and even in most classrooms. He didn't notice a great deal of tension between the two groups (poverty cut across racial lines and was the big equalizer) but they rarely, if ever, mixed.

The split bugged him: in part, because he knew that these kids could get more out of their experiences and because they could become a better team if they learned to get along well, not to mention trust and respect one another. He solved it by insisting that whenever and wherever the team met, the players would group themselves by class or by position. On the field, in the locker room, or on the bus, that's how players sat. The Raiders were 2-28-1 in the three years prior to Purzycki's arrival. They went 15-12-3 in his three years as coach. In his final season (1974), they played Caesar Rodney High School (CRHS), the state's second-largest school, from the Dover suburb of Camden. Woodbridge prevailed in a shocking upset that eventually led to a coaching change. Caesar Rodney's administration decided that they wanted the guy who had led that little Woodbridge High program to success ... and they hired Purzycki.

It was during his time at CRHS that Purzycki started to make a name for himself as a coach. In three years, the Riders didn't lose a regular season game, and in 1975 Purzycki was named the state high school coach of the year when his team became the first downstate school ever to win a Delaware high school football championship.

That 1975 CRHS team drew powerful Saint Mark's of Wilmington in the first round of the playoffs. Saint Mark's was heavily favored to win its third straight state championship.

Purzycki's biggest strength in coaching has always been motivation, and the day of the Saint Mark's game he found a way to push the right button for every one of his players.

Saint Mark's only loss on the season was to their arch-rival Salesianum and since that defeat they had been counting on getting revenge in the playoffs. But, before they played Purzycki's squad, everyone found out Salesianum had been defeated by Newark High in the other semi-final game. When the score was announced, Purzycki detected frustration from the Saint Mark's players. Their revenge game wasn't going to happen. Back in the locker room before kickoff, Purzycki hit upon what he perceived as a slight to his team.

"Did you see those guys?" he yelled. "They've already planned on beating you and now they're mad that they won't get to play their rival again. They don't even know you're here!"

The Riders won the semifinal game, 22-14, and went on to beat Newark High the next week, 18-14, to claim the Delaware state championship.

"We took great pride in being the first team from downstate to win a title," he said. "The people north of the canal always tended to look down upon the teams from the south."

To supplement his teaching income at Caesar Rodney, he spent his summers running a playground for the county recreation department in Star Hill, one of the most impoverished neighborhoods in Dover. The kids were almost all poor and almost all black. Playing with the kids and talking to their parents each day over the course of three summers allowed him to develop the kind of personal and emotional relationships that he now believed was the key to better understanding between races.

He had come a long way from hanging out at the Dairy Queen on South Orange Avenue.

Purzycki's CRHS teams were 33-and-2 in his three seasons and that success got him a lot of recognition. State officials were so impressed they awarded him with the Order of the First State, which is the highest civilian honor that can be given in Delaware. It was presented to him at a ceremony by Governor Pete DuPont. He also got a job offer (which he took) from Tubby Raymond to join the staff at the University of Delaware.

What's more, the success he had at CRHS was noticed by the athletic director at the nearby University of Maryland Eastern Shore; a gentleman named Nelson Townsend.

TWELVE

Purzycki's second meeting with his new team went better than the first.

When he arrived on campus for his first full week of work, Townsend told him that he'd sent a letter to every player informing them that there was a meeting with the new coach. He left no ambiguity in the letter. If you wanted to play football at Delaware State in 1981 and keep your scholarship, you would attend the meeting.

Most of the players did.

Of those who didn't some had long ago decided to quit the team. They had grown weary of the game and perhaps of Del State's inability to be any good at it, so they were already done. Certainly, some others skipped the meeting as an ongoing protest. Their status would be iffy at best.

But when Purzycki walked into the meeting, at least he had a room full of players ready to listen to what he had to say.

His first move was to ask all non-players, including Townsend, to please leave. Managers, support staff, trainers, and the athletic director headed for the door. When it closed, it was just Purzycki and his team. There were no handouts. No plans outlining an easy road to success. Purzycki spoke from his heart.

"Look, guys, I understand the situation," he began. "I think I understand how you feel. Willie Jeffries at Wichita State and Denny Green at Northwestern. That's it. That's all the black head coaches currently working in Division I outside of the Historic Black College and University network. It's not right. There should be more and there will be more. But I can't do anything about that. I don't have any agenda here other than to coach you guys. I came here because I have a passion to be a head football coach. I want to lead this team and I want to make you a great team."

Purzycki paused for a moment and looked around the room. During team speeches, he had a tendency to get emotional and he was doing his best to keep that side of his personality in check.

"I've talked to guys who are going to join my staff and they think the same thing I do. They think Delaware State is a sleeping giant. I want you to have success. I want this place to be special. Guys, I want to make this place the Grambling of the east."

Purzycki was sincere if not pushing the envelope a bit. Grambling was THE powerhouse program among HBCU schools. Coached by legendary Eddie Robinson, the Tigers of upstate Louisiana had just won their ninth conference championship in the past 10 years. Every player in the room knew about Grambling State College. Purzycki paused again and looked into their eyes. No one scoffed at the idea of trying to become an East Coast version of Grambling.

"Here are my rules:

"I'm never going to lie or misrepresent myself to you, ever. I'm asking you to do the same. If we're straight with each other then we'll trust each other. And if we trust each other, we can do anything together.

"If I have to go out and play with a roster of all freshman, I'll do it if you guys choose not to be here. But from today forward we're not concerning ourselves with who is not here. We're moving on and we're going to build something special."

Those were the rules. Purzycki then informed them that they were required to be in the school's new weight room at 6:00 a.m. sharp every Monday, Wednesday, and Friday for team weightlifting sessions.

"That starts immediately," he said, wrapping up the meeting.

"He gave us his vision for the school and how things were going to change moving forward," said Matt Horace. "I remember he had a very business-like approach to football, which none of us had ever seen before, certainly not at Del State."

"He had a strong presence about himself," said Terry Staples. "He was really excited about the chance to coach at Delaware State. He had that fiery way of speaking and he commanded the room. He convinced me that he really wanted to get this thing going and I'm sure he also wanted to prove himself because he knew everybody was against him."

Walt Samuels, Thunder Thornton, and Calvin Mason were entering their fifth year at the school. Purzycki would be their third head coach so they had heard plenty of speeches. This one felt different.

"It was refreshing to hear his passion and that allowed me to feel like I was on board," said Samuels. "I didn't pay any attention to the ones who were disgruntled. I knew we had talent on the team and I was interested in helping turn things around."

Thornton called it "A whole different approach to football and a better attitude towards the game. I embraced it immediately and was happy about the change."

"Give him credit," said Mason. "He had the mindset to see a little bit farther than a lot of the other coaches who had been there before him on how to implement a plan and move the program forward."

But there was still plenty of cynicism. Purzycki opened some eyes that day but he didn't win over everyone. "At that point, some people were still skeptical," said Horace. "It was kind of like, 'Yeah, whatever. Let's see what happens.'"

Quarterback Sam Warren saw both sides of the argument. He was a self-described football geek who knew all about Tubby Raymond and the great success of Delaware football. Warren realized that Townsend's plan in hiring Purzycki was to see if he could bring a little of that magic to Dover. But he also saw the other side of the story.

"I understood the HBCU thing. Some of the guys were grumbling that just because we had one bad season we had to hire a white coach. They felt like the school gave up on us."

In truth, it was exactly the opposite. Townsend and the trustees were willing to do anything – even risking widespread alienation to NOT give up on the team.

Purzycki recognized that much of the work in front of him had little to do with football itself. He joked with friends that he had taken a job at a school "that had a locker room with no lockers, a stadium with no fans, and a weight room with no weights."

He was able to get a weight training program going because Townsend had made it a priority and found money somewhere to buy new weights. "I told Nelson I didn't need much," Purzycki said. "Get us some basic Olympic weights and we'll make men out of these guys."

Not every player loves lifting weights but for the ones who did, the room brought out their competitive fire. "They created a 1,000-pound club," Staples said. "They put up charts, so you could see where you ranked on the team. That created competition because you naturally wanted to get better. Before, you'd go in there, crack a few jokes, and leave. Now, we were creating something. We started thinking 'I can't wait to get into that weight room. I'm gonna get my squats up.'"

Townsend and Purzycki continued to bond largely due to the fact that Purzycki didn't know anyone else on campus. His assistant coaches wouldn't be hired until July so for the first few months, he was a staff of one. Sociable by nature, it wore him down to constantly be alone. He was also finding out how it can feel to be in the minority.

"No one was being openly disrespectful," he said, "but no one would engage me, either. The isolation I was feeling was painful to me." He was beginning to understand how black people – even those he'd known in seemingly comfortable situations (at least to him) – often suffered in all-white environments. He just found it so lonely.

Adding to Purzycki's angst was the continued presence at Del State of the coaching staff that had been fired to make way for him. Charles Henderson and his assistants all had contracts that ran through June 30th and had been reassigned to other duties at DSC. Henderson was interviewed by the *Delaware State News* about the player and student reaction to Purzycki's hiring and being honest with his feelings did the new coach no favors.

"I think the kids are aware that there are some black coaches who are more qualified than Joe Purzycki, or anybody in the final group of candidates," Henderson said. "I think the key is these kids may feel we have come a long way and why throw the shock of a new head coach who is white on us now? Let's face it, they're aware of the structure of the country and just lean toward a black coach. I think some people are ready for a white coach but talking about Delaware State as a total thing … I think they are not ready. It's going to take people a while to swallow it."

Henderson also tied the player's feelings to the emerging effort to turn Martin Luther King's birthday into a national holiday. "The kids are involved with the hassle going on to set a special day aside for Martin Luther King," he said. "They are experiencing feelings like this and it has an effect on them."

Purzycki endorsed the creation of a holiday for Dr. King and was bewildered that Henderson had tried to link it to his hiring.

Henderson's voice obviously still had some weight on campus, which was small enough that Purzycki was constantly bumping into him or one of his former assistants. It wasn't unusual for Hornet players who were still unsure what to make of Purzycki to discuss their feelings with their former coaches. Purzycki shook his head when he imagined what those players were being told and often felt like he was walking through a sea of side-eyes.

Purzycki sat and talked with Townsend every day during those first weeks, and one day when the AD asked him how things were going, he opened up about his anxiety.

"I feel like I'm invisible on campus," Purzycki said. "There's constant silence when I'm around and I'm being ignored. It's like I'm not even there."

"Well, go have lunch in the cafeteria," Townsend responded. "They'll warm up to you and you'll get some of the people to come over and sit with you."

Townsend was trying to be encouraging but his words only served to increase Purzycki's frustration. "I've tried that and I'm telling you, when I walk through the campus here, it's like the sea parts."

Townsend's tone quickly changed, much like when Purzycki told him on his first day on the job that he wasn't sure things were going to work out.

"What the –" he sputtered. "Do you have any idea of what my people have been through, and you're worried because you got a little bit ignored? My people have gone through a lot more than this. I knew one thing about this situation and that is if I hired a white coach for this job he had to be really tough to get through all this stuff. You've gotta be tough, Joe. You've gotta toughen up."

"Nelson, I hear you," Purzycki replied. "And I've got the courage. But I feel like an invisible man. The last thing any black student on campus wants is to be seen with me."

Purzycki didn't even realize he was identifying sentiments from Ralph Ellison's influential novel, "Invisible Man," journaling a young black man's awakening to racial discrimination, published in 1952:

"I am an invisible man. … I am a man of substance, of flesh and bone, fiber and liquids – and I might even be said to possess a mind. I am invisible, understand, simply because people refuse to see me …"

Townsend knew. Purzycki was learning.

Townsend ended their discussion by informing Purzycki that the following day they were going to walk into the cafeteria together and have lunch. That's it. They were going to sit down and have lunch together. And somehow, someway, Purzycki had to trust Townsend, it just might help. At least a little.

Purzycki appreciated Townsend's bluntness and the dose of perspective, even though he wasn't used to having his toughness questioned. He also was skeptical that students, many of whom were still upset with his hiring, would suddenly warm up to him because he was having lunch with the AD.

At noon the next day, Townsend announced himself at Purzycki's office door with a commanding, "Let's go!" They walked over to the cafeteria, filled their trays, sat down, and started eating. They were a few bites in when Purzycki pointed out the obvious.

"You'll notice," he said to Townsend with a smile. "You don't see a whole lot of people coming over here to sit with us, do you?"

Townsend had indeed noticed, and he was there to do something about it. He started calling out various students by name and inviting them to come over: "Do you know Coach Purzycki? Come over here. Sit down, join us, and visit with us while we have lunch."

The students all knew and liked Townsend, so at his encouragement, they were willing to spend a few minutes at least acting like they were getting to know the new guy on campus. Purzycki's personality took over and before long he was talking with several students. One lunch wasn't going to fix everything, but it cheered the new coach to be engaged in conversation.

"It's like he was recruiting kids to come over and sit with us," Purzycki said. "It was another example to me of how invested he was in me and how bad he would have looked if I didn't work out. We were joined inextricably together in this journey. He needed me, and I needed him."

They parted ways after lunch and as he walked back to his office Purzycki was struck by the way Townsend had become part of the solution to the problem using nothing more than the sheer force of his personality.

"This guy," Purzycki thought to himself, "is a real man."

Another more-than-suggestion from Townsend: "You gotta go to the basketball games. It'll help you gain acceptance."

A few nights later when he attended a Del State basketball game, Purzycki walked into the lobby at halftime and took up what had become a familiar position: standing awkwardly by himself in a room full of people who ignored him. But a young woman made eye contact with him.

Velda Bowles, was one of the most popular girls on campus and significantly her boyfriend (punter Clyde Alderman) was on the football team, and she had a big smile on her face as she walked over to introduce herself.

"Welcome to Del State," she said warmly. "How are things going? Clyde told me you met with the team and it was a good meeting."

Purzycki and his new friend made small talk for a few minutes before the second half. As she walked back to her friends, Purzycki felt his heart warmed by this small but friendly gesture.

"It was incredibly courageous for her to do that," he said. "She told me later that she didn't think it was courageous. She was just being herself. She didn't view me as the enemy or the guy no one wanted to be there."

A meticulous notetaker, Purzycki wrote in his nightly journal that Bowles' visit "broke the ice for me."

He later looked back and recalled that "A lot of people saw her talking to me and that incident began a measure of acceptability that made each day go a little easier and better. I felt like her visit was a big step forward for me."

Little by little, he was becoming more visible.

Purzycki had at least one more fan in those early days. Diane Townsend liked him from the moment they met. Before hiring

Purzycki, Nelson made the unusual gesture of inviting Purzycki to his house for dinner.

"He usually wanted me to meet people he was considering hiring," Diane Townsend said. "But we always did it in a restaurant. Joe was the only guy he ever had come to our house."

The dinner happened before anyone knew Purzycki was a candidate, and in a reversal of the script of the 1967 Academy Award-winning movie *Guess Who's Coming to Dinner*, Diane Townsend didn't know Purzycki was white until she answered the door that evening.

She said she wasn't shocked but admitted thinking to herself, "OK. Alright." as Purzycki came into the house. Within minutes, his charm assuaged any doubts she had.

"I remember sitting at the kitchen table with Joe and talking about stuff," she said. "I never got the impression that he was afraid or uncomfortable. He felt like someone we had known for a long time. He didn't feel like a stranger and he didn't act like a stranger. He was such a pleasant guy and I liked how it felt having him in my house."

She also admired his willingness to take the job. "For Nelson to hire him was one thing, but it took a different kind of courage from Joe to accept that job and subject himself and his family to that pressure. He was taking a big chance."

In addition to bluntness and wisdom, Townsend used humor to add levity to potentially uncomfortable situations he and his new coach sometimes encountered. Shortly after Purzycki was hired, Townsend told him about the President's Ball at Delaware State.

"It's the biggest function of the year, it's formal, and you've got to attend," Townsend said. "The entire faculty of the college will be there. This isn't going to be easy for you and Sharon because a lot of people who will be there aren't overly enthusiastic that we hired you."

Not overly enthusiastic. Right.

The Purzyckis arrived at Townsend's house the night of the ball. Sharon and Diane had not met, and introductions were made. In the course of the conversation, Townsend could tell his new coach was extremely nervous about the evening.

"Relax," he said to Purzycki. "Here's what we're going to do."

"We're gonna walk in like this ... and we're gonna look at everybody and say, 'That's right! We bad! We bad!'"

It was right from a famous scene of the number one movie in America at the time – *Stir Crazy*. In the film, Richard Pryor and Gene Wilder were framed for a bank robbery, and Pryor is giving Wilder advice on how to act cool walking into prison for the first time.

Suddenly, in the middle of his living room, Townsend was channeling Pryor's exaggerated hipster walk and talk. "That's right, that's right!" They were going to walk in and take over.

It broke them up, and while there were still awkward moments for the Purzyckis during the evening, Townsend's humor served the desired effect to relax everyone, particularly Purzycki. They'd already developed a bond stronger than the typical AD/coach relationship.

"They became close because of the situation," Diane Townsend said. "Nelson was closer to Joe than he was with any other coach. They had a lot of respect for each other."

THIRTEEN

Purzycki was making some progress as days one the job turned into weeks on the job. His players weren't fans of the 6 a.m. weight training sessions ("They hated getting up that early and I had to constantly browbeat everybody who wasn't showing up."). Yet, most players were showing up and the coach was learning about the individual personalities on his team.

"Getting a weight room felt like a huge step up," said Anthony Sharpe, who was a junior that season. "When I got to Delaware State all we had was heart. We didn't have a weight room. We didn't have anything. There were a lot of guys like me who just wanted to get the program in order and Purzycki didn't have to win us over."

Sharpe emerged as an early team leader in Purzycki's tenure. He was the first person in his family to go to college and sure wasn't going to lose his scholarship over something as petty as the color of his new coach's skin. He could tell the new guy knew what he was doing. "By the time you're playing college football, you've played a lot of football. You know what works and what doesn't."

Players attending early morning weight training sessions clearly wanted to be a part of the turnaround. But then, they would leave the team environment and find themselves back on campus with students and a rising list of former players whose primary currency when it came to Del State football was negativity. Similar to the summers during Purzycki's college years when he would feel himself getting sucked back into the intolerance of some of the people in his neighborhood, it took work on the part of his players to not be influenced by the opposition on campus.

"Early on it was tough for him to get the students on his side," said Matt Horace, another player who bought into what Purzycki was selling. "There's always a lot of group-think on a college campus. There was talk that Purzycki's arrival meant Del State was going to be closed and merged with the University of Delaware. People were concerned because they thought all this stuff was happening."

People who felt that way got all the ammo they needed to fuel their fears from the DSC student newspaper, the *Hornet*. Campus newspapers traditionally operate on the margins. They generally print the truth, but being run by college students, those ideals are often filtered through a certain brand of irreverence, humor, and passion. From the day he was hired, the *Hornet* staked out an anti-Purzycki stance.

A January 27th story headlined "New Coach Triggers Old Problems" claimed that "the general consensus is that Purzycki was not the most qualified for the job and the whole issue was a racist one. A large sector of the DSC community believes that Billy Joe is the better man for the job."

That same issue had a letter to the editor in which an anonymous student criticized the Board of Trustees. "Not once did they consider what the players wanted. Instead, they chose a 'Polish Prince' to lead the black fold on to victory." Purzycki was a little taken aback that his heritage was being mocked by the student paper.

An uncredited editorial on February 24th stoked the fires of fear that Purzycki's arrival was the Trojan Horse that would destroy Delaware State's very identity.

"You may think things don't pertain to you but when Del State College hired a white high school football coach over a black and more qualified assistant pro football coach it pertains to you. It will affect you when you come back to your alma mater and the football team is predominantly white. When you come back five or ten years from now and the predominantly black Del State you used to know is annexed to the U of D and predominantly white, will it pertain to you then?"

The paper proclaimed that Purzycki's staff would be all-white and that he had been given an unlimited recruiting budget. The paper was distributed throughout the campus and it was impossible for Purzycki to ignore. The continued attacks felt personal.

One night, Purzycki was working late when he was suddenly startled by several voices just outside his office window. He looked out and saw several young men jumping up and down and yelling.

Purzycki couldn't make out what the guys outside his window were saying but it unnerved him a bit. "I wondered if they were yelling at me," he admitted. He left the office soon after and went home for the day.

The next morning, he stopped by Townsend's office. "Nelson, there were a bunch of guys standing right outside my window last night yelling and chanting things. Do you know anything about that?"

Townsend smiled at Purzycki and told him not to worry about it. "That's just a bunch of kids pledging fraternities on campus. They've got some things they have to say and songs they have to sing, and they were just doing that. It's nothing."

Purzycki shrugged his shoulders and left Townsend's office to head to his own. He knew he was still unpopular among a contingent of the DSC student body but after talking to Townsend he was willing to admit that perhaps his paranoia was getting the best of him. Then he got to his office and opened the door.

"There was glass everywhere," he said. "The window to the office had been shattered by a brick that sat on the floor. My papers were scattered all over the room, the file cabinet drawers were opened, and the entire room was a mess." He went back to Townsend and told him what happened. Before long, Townsend, Purzycki, and campus security personnel were standing in the office trying to figure things out.

"Nelson, in his wisdom, didn't want this incident to be construed as a personal attack against me," Purzycki said. "He and the security people quickly concluded that this was the work of random vandals."

Purzycki was shocked.

"Nelson," he said, "I'm no dummy. My office just got ransacked. There are bricks on the floor and broken glass everywhere. There are footprints on the desk. This wasn't random." Townsend didn't want to debate the obvious with Purzycki, so he brought things to a close by declaring that he was moving Purzycki to a new office on the second floor.

"It was a much nicer office, my staff ended up right outside my office in a big room with a light hanging down that swung back and forth. We joked that it looked like someplace you'd conduct an interrogation."

As for the vandalism at his now-abandoned first office? "Nothing came of it and Nelson and I never discussed it again."

Purzycki didn't have time to focus on who was against him, anyway, since he had to find guys who wanted to play for him. Purzycki's late hiring date left him scrambling to find players who had talent but had not committed to other schools.

Recruiting is hard enough under the best of circumstances. When you're behind everyone else, and with all the baggage at Del State that year, it was even tougher. Even more, Purzycki was still a solo act unable to pay coaches to join him until July. But that didn't prevent Herky Billings, who had reached an agreement to join Purzycki at Del State, from helping out.

Although the *Hornet* maintained he'd been given an unlimited recruiting budget, the truth was, he was allotted $300 his first year. Purzycki needed all the help he could get. "I love Herky," he said. "On his own dime and his own time, he went out that first year and helped me recruit."

Compared to Delaware's recruiting budget of $50,000, the budget was laughable. There would come a day when it would be increased, and he'd eventually get to hire assistant coaches, but for that first year, Purzycki didn't have time to fret about it. Part of his plan to enjoy sustained success was to stop recruiting so many players from Florida and Georgia and instead focus on kids who lived within a couple hours of Delaware State. They'd be less likely to get homesick, and their families and friends would be more likely to come to the games. That he was working with pennies against the dollar that first spring didn't overwhelm him.

"When we found a kid who was interested, I'd get them to come to campus with his family," Purzycki said. "I had a lot of upper-classmen, guys like Sam Warren, Tim King, Marvin Blount, Thunder Thornton, and Anthony Sharpe who had shown a belief in me. I'd get one of them to tour the recruit and his family around campus."

Purzycki had specific instructions for the tours. He wanted recruits to see the good side of DSC, so he insisted his players take them to the newer, nicer, dormitory. They'd see the library and the dining hall. He and Townsend were working on a way to get money to get actual lockers for the locker room, but that hadn't happened yet.

"Do not," he told his tour-guide players, "take them to the locker room. Tell them it's under construction."

He loved having Billings around. He knew football, could spot talent, and was quick with a joke or a laugh. At an all-star game in Philadelphia, Billings and Purzycki were standing together watching the game and trying to find players.

"It was a little like being at a horse race," Billings said. "We were just looking at guys, seeing them for the first time, and guessing whether they might be able to play for us."

After a few minutes, a guy walked up and asked them a question. "Hey, are you two guys datin'?"

"What?" Billings responded. "What did you just say?"

"I asked if you guys are from the University of Dayton," came the reply. Purzycki and Billings were both wearing red hats with a blue D on them. They roared with laughter as they explained that, no, they weren't Dayton. They were Delaware State.

At one point that spring, Purzycki got a tip about a player named Joe Lane who played for the high school (Vailsburg) Purzycki had originally attended in Newark. They met and according to Lane, "really connected because he was so down to Earth with me."

Purzycki then unwittingly almost blew a chance to get Lane to play for him at Del State. "After we met, I left school and walked out to a bus stop," Lane said. "It was freezing cold that day, and I looked up and there went Coach Purzycki zooming by in his car."

Stuck waiting for a bus in the biting cold Lane decided that he wasn't going to Del State because Purzycki hadn't offered him a ride. Eventually, he realized the coach likely didn't see him, and since he wanted to play close to home an offer from Del State was worth taking.

Billings wasn't so lucky recruiting a different New Jersey player. They had a good visit and Billings left the kid's house thinking he had a found a guy who wanted to help them build something. A few days later he followed up with a phone call and asked the kid if he wanted to come to Del State.

"Coach," he said, "I've got to be honest with you. I've been talking with Army and I think that's where I'm going to go."

Billings was disappointed but that's how recruiting sometimes goes. "When we talked at your house," he said to the kid, "you never even mentioned that Army was recruiting you. They've got a good program. It could be a good fit for you."

"No, coach," the kid replied. "You don't understand. I'm not going to play football at Army. I'm going to enlist in the Army."

Billings was dumbfounded. They were offering him a full scholarship to go to college and he was going to enlist in the Army instead. "That's where we were that first spring," he said. "That's part of what we were up against."

But there were successes, too. Purzycki and Billings could tell that their prior association with Delaware was going to help them. "We were two of Tubby's own," Purzycki said. "That was viewed as a positive in most homes. We had both played and coached in some great success at Delaware, which led to a feeling among parents that we would take care of their sons. And since many high schools in the area used it, the fact that we were planning on running the Delaware Wing-T was also viewed as a huge positive"

"Joe and I had been winners every place we had ever been," Billings said. "And that's the attitude we showed recruits and their parents. We were going to win at Del State, too."

Purzycki's found it interesting that what was viewed by some at Del State as a negative (the Delaware connection) was helping open doors to new recruits in the region. In addition to finding players, he was meeting with others who wanted to join his staff. He had settled on Bill Collick (who also provided recruiting assistance that first spring) as his defensive coordinator. He heard from an area coach named Bill Huntstock who wanted to join his staff. Purzycki set up a meeting with Huntstock and told Townsend about it in passing.

"Take a car from the school's motor pool," Townsend said. "That will save you some money."

Purzycki reserved a car for that afternoon. As he approached the intersection where the diner where he was to meet Huntstock was located, he slowed down. The brakes on the car had been a little mushy since he left Dover, so he was driving cautiously.

"I approached a red light near the diner and when I hit the brakes the pedal went straight to the floor," he said. "I steered over to the shoulder of the road and coasted right through the red light. I pulled the emergency brake, which helped a little. I was probably still going about 20 miles per hour when I decided to turn into the diner's parking lot."

Purzycki frantically steered his careening car away from others in the lot and went barreling around the side of the building. He finally brought his runaway car to a thudding stop by crashing it into a guardrail that protected a grassy area behind the restaurant. He called the motor pool and told them where they could find the car; his meeting with Huntstock turned into Huntstock giving him a ride back to campus where he met with Townsend.

"I think someone cut the brake lines on the car," Purzycki said.

"What do you mean someone cut the brake lines?" Townsend said. "You said they worked fine when you left."

"Yeah but I kept having to push the brake harder to make it work, and then finally I pushed all the way to the floor and the car wouldn't stop. I'm not making this up. Come on, Nelson, I wouldn't take a motor pool car and crash it in the back of a diner."

The next day, Townsend told him the mechanic at the motor pool checked the car and concluded it was only a leak caused by normal wear. There was nothing sinister about it. Nevertheless, Purzycki never took a car from the DSC motor pool again.

Purzycki recognized that the entire thing was just a coincidence, but he was having trouble managing his growing paranoia.

"You're imagining things," Townsend said.

"Yeah," Purzycki answered, "but I'm imagining things that are happening to me."

FOURTEEN

Finally, spring football began: Purzycki could put a whistle around his neck and start working with his players on the practice field.

Coaches love spring ball because they get a chance to coach and teach players without having to also get ready for an opponent each week. In Purzycki's case, it also allowed him to put some of the craziness aside and focus on what he was there for.

Sixty-one players hit the field with their new coach on March 30th. A total of 17 scholarship players had quit since Purzycki had been hired, including several with experience who would have made his job easier if they had stayed. Not everyone quit simply because of the new coach. "Some guys just felt they didn't have it in them to play football anymore," Purzycki told the *Delaware State News*.

In that same story, several players demonstrated that Purzycki's personality and strengths as a football coach had won them over. "Our coach let us know if we don't want to be on the practice field we should let him know now," said quarterback Sam Warren. "Anyone who is out here today is here because they want to be."

Senior defensive back Tim King downplayed the on-campus controversy of the past two months. "It was just a lot of non-football players who were doing all the talking. It was people who had nothing to do with the team, people who don't suit up on Saturdays."

But, those people were still talking.

The arrival of organized workouts was reported by the *Hornet* in what had become typical fashion. A story that contained nothing more than basic info (when practice was, how many players were out, the Red-Blue Game schedule) was given the headline "Bleak Future for Hornets."

Typical of any football team, there were players who weren't 100 percent on-board with the new coach and the new systems he was installing, but four workouts each week made it easy to see who those guys were and allowed coaches to work with them and try to improve those attitudes.

"I think the biggest difference this year," Warren said, "is that the coaches are more like teachers. Practice is another class and if you're not paying attention, they'll know."

Another big difference was the national attention Purzycki's hiring was attracting at Delaware State. The *New York Times* ran a story on the Hornets on April 6th reporting that the players were "working vigorously to try and turn things around" under their new coach.

In the story, Townsend talked about the hiring and his vision for the future. "As blacks, we are cognizant of blacks having a chance to go to white schools. But in a way, we were speaking with forked tongues. Why shouldn't a qualified white coach be a candidate at a black school? Besides that, I am interested in building a program that will outlast Purzycki or Townsend. We've got that type person in Joe and he's done a tremendous job so far."

Purzycki acknowledged the significance of his hiring as well: "I am hoping people will see how a tiny Delaware school took a courageous step. Maybe a lot of people can learn from this."

As the spring workouts progressed, Purzycki started getting his legs under him. "There were still people still trying to undermine the progress we were making," he said, "but as I met with guys and they were around me more often I began getting confidence in my ability to make it work."

Purzycki also now had guys around him he knew and trusted. Billings and Collick were helping him with spring football, as was a guy who became a valuable asset. Really, he was a gift from Nelson Townsend.

"I know you want to choose your own staff," Townsend said in a meeting with Purzycki in February. "But I'm going to suggest you hire a guy named Walter Tullis as one of your assistant coaches."

Tullis was a Del State legend who played wide receiver for the Hornets in the mid-seventies and was good enough to spend two seasons with Green Bay in the NFL. He also had been an All-

American track star for Del State and Townsend had hired him to be the school's track coach. He counseled Purzycki that Tullis could help him in a very direct way.

"He can go into the dorms and talk to the players in a way you can't right now," Townsend said. "Meet with him and see what you think." Purzycki got the feeling Townsend was telling him to hire Tullis and in many situations that kind of directive from an athletic director creates problems. But by now, Purzycki trusted Townsend: If Townsend thought Tullis was a good idea, Purzycki figured he was probably a good idea.

"He drove onto campus in a huge Cadillac and was dressed to the nines the first time we met," Purzycki recalled. "He turns out to be one of the nicest men I've ever known. I could tell he'd be a great fit and I knew Nelson was right. I needed his help."

"What's this bullshit that these guys won't give you a chance?" Tullis said to Purzycki in their first meeting. "To hell with that. I'll take care of them. I'll straighten them out." Tullis's success as an athlete gave him credibility with the football team. He spent time with players in the dorms, in the weight room, and in the dining hall. He was able to sort out who was with Purzycki and who was against him.

"He'd come into the dorm and talk to players," said Calvin Mason. "He told us about some of the things Purzycki and Townsend were planning to do and how good things were going to be."

"Look, guys," Tullis often said to skeptical players, "You've got somebody here who wants to take this program to a new level."

"In the first two months on the job, I was on an island," Purzycki said. "Walter was one of the first guys to take my back. He provided loyalty and strength to me and became critically important to our success."

As spring practice continued, players could tell Purzycki and his staff knew what they were doing. Practices were organized and there were small but encouraging signs of progress.

"Before, we never knew what we going to do from minute to minute or day to day," said Matt Horace. "When Coach Purzycki came in we had a schedule every day. Here's what we're doing from 2:00 to 2:20. Here's what we're doing from 2:20 to 2:40. It was organization that we really needed."

"Purzycki was great at motivating people," said Calvin Mason. "He was very good at seeing the vision and explaining the 'why' behind his decisions."

Mason was a big defensive lineman who would become one of Purzycki's favorites. He was a Florida native and if his teammates thought practice was hard he would regale them with stories of tough summer days working in an orange grove during the summer.

"You carried a big ladder and a sack and spent all day filling the sack up with grapefruits, tangerines, and oranges," he said. "And you had to watch out for all kinds of animals in the fruit grove. Wild hogs. Raccoons. And snakes." Mason would tell his teammates that most of the animals could be dealt with but that "when the rattlesnakes show up, it's quittin' time!"

Purzycki loved Mason. He was the kind of big, experienced player who could help the team, he had a great sense of humor, and he was a natural leader. But Mason was one of the instigators of the original student protests on the day Purzycki was hired and he wasn't sure how the new coach felt about that or him. So, he avoided speaking to him. A few weeks into spring ball Purzycki approached him on the field.

"How come you haven't come by my office to talk to me?" Purzycki asked. "Most of the other players have stopped in. I want you to come see me, so we can talk and get to know each other."

"I wasn't sure if you wanted to talk to me after all the stuff that went on," Mason replied.

Purzycki thought back to his childhood in Newark. He was raised in a huge extended family of passionate, demonstrative people who sometimes clashed over matters big and small. He'd seen (and participated in) some wild arguments between relatives growing up, but family love was always stronger than any disagreement and people didn't stay mad at each other for long.

"Calvin, that's all in the past," Purzycki said. "We're a family here in this football program and we will always come together."

Before long Mason stopped by Purzycki's office.

"We started talking and I come to find out that I was totally wrong about the way I thought he felt about me," Mason said, "and we were off and running from that point on."

Fullback Richard Williams was another player who was slowly being won over by the new coach. Like Mason, Williams was vocal in his displeasure when Purzycki's hiring was announced.

"It had nothing to do with his skin color," Williams said. "I spoke out against him because I couldn't believe that a guy with Billy Joe's credentials was being passed over. You looked at what he had done, and you looked at what Purzycki had done, and it just didn't make sense to me."

Purzycki got help from Townsend on that issue. Williams said that at one point after the hiring he and a group of players were informally talking to the athletic director when the subject of Purzycki's lack of experience came up.

"Let me explain something to you," Townsend told the players. "Purzycki didn't have as much experience, but he had a plan for what he wanted to do here. The other guys had experience, but if they had a plan, they didn't share it with us. Let that be a lesson to you guys. Prepare for the things you want in life."

Williams and some of his teammates may have remained skeptical about how things would work out, but after that conversation they had a better understanding of Townsend's decision.

Spring ball concluded with the Red-Blue game, after which Purzycki told Wasser he was pleased with his team. "Actually, I didn't think we'd be as far along as we are. I've still got to be patient. Some things we're doing are going to take time."

Thunder Thornton was even more enthusiastic than his coach. He'd seen a transformation from within the team and was excited about his senior season. "The biggest difference between this year and last is there aren't any arguments in the huddle. Everyone knew what he had to do and did it. If somebody missed a tackle last year, everybody would get all over him in the huddle. We didn't have any of that today."

When spring practice ended Purzycki took some satisfaction in what he and his staff had accomplished to that point. There would still be challenges, but he had a nucleus of guys who were committed to improving Del State football.

As players left campus to enjoy their summer vacations, Purzycki and his staff got down to business. It was mid-June and they had a lot of work to do before their first season. Some of that work cost money they simply didn't have. The budget for football would eventually be increased but Townsend had made it clear from the start that Purzycki at first was going to have to do more with less. Purzycki was always telling his staff they had to be creative about the lack of funds.

As luck would have it, Independence Day fell on a Saturday in 1981 which meant on Friday, there would be an unending procession of cars heading down Highway 13 toward Delaware beaches. The highway ran right past Delaware State and Bill Collick saw a fund-raising opportunity.

"Chicken Ed," Collick told Purzycki. "He has the most popular chicken stand in the area and he's willing to give us enough chickens so that we can hold a big barbecue. We can do it on the Friday before the holiday on the lawn in front of the school, we'll sell chicken to people heading to the beach, and we'll take all the profits for the football program."

Purzycki knew all about Chicken Ed and agreed that his secret sauce made his chicken legendary. When Collick told him that the barbecue sauce was part of the deal, Purzycki was all in. The staff agreed to help out and the intrepid chicken salesmen hoped to raise at least $1,000 for the football team.

"We put big signs out on the highway to let people know what we were doing," Purzycki said. "We had a great, well-thought-out plan. But then two cops show up and tell us we don't have a permit for the signs and they can't be on the highway. So, we're standing next to a busy highway all day, but no one knows what we're doing, and no one is coming into our chicken barbecue."

They sold a grand total of four chicken dinners. By the end of the day they were depressed and had reached two conclusions: They were all going to be eating chicken for the foreseeable future and they were powerfully thirsty. The remedy for that last problem was located just across the highway.

Highway 13 was the busiest road in the state and on holiday weekends police would set the stoplights to run for extended periods of green to allow traffic to get by. Getting to the beer store across the highway in the sea of cars zooming past their ill-fated fundraiser was a fool's errand no one was willing to take. Roger Hunt was the DSC trainer and had been on the chicken-selling crew.

"I'll go get us some beer," he told the coaches. They weren't sure what his plan was, but Hunt set off in the direction of the school's stadium.

"A few minutes later," Purzycki said, "Here comes this ambulance with lights and siren both on and Roger behind the wheel. He gave us a thumbs-up as he drove past us across six lanes of suddenly stopped traffic."

Purzycki and his staff were laughing at the spectacle. DSC owned an ambulance to transport injured athletes to a city hospital. That ambulance was now parked in front of a liquor store as Hunt hurried in to buy beer.

"A few minutes later," Purzycki said, "Roger comes running out with the beer and gets in the ambulance. He turns the siren back on, stops traffic again, and comes across the busy highway back to where we were."

The coaching staff was admiring Hunt's chutzpah when two Delaware State Police cars suddenly turned off the highway with *their* lights and sirens on. Purzycki said his first thought upon seeing the police was succinct.

"Oh, shit."

Hunt immediately fell on his sword. "It's my fault," he told the police. "I did it. I know I shouldn't have run the siren. I know it was wrong."

The police were not amused but after a few minutes decided to let the incident slide, which was the best news Purzycki had received all day.

"After everything we'd been through," he said with a laugh, "I couldn't imagine having to call Nelson on a holiday weekend and explain that we had turned the school's ambulance into a beer wagon and we were all in jail."

The Hornets' season opener at Virginia State was nine weeks away.

FIFTEEN

West Philadelphia native Eldridge "Ace" Comer had been in Dover for less than 10 minutes when he decided he wanted to leave.

Comer was a quick running back who Purzycki and Billings had spotted at the all-star game they attended in Philadelphia. They agreed that Comer could perfectly fit their offense, and they offered him a scholarship that day.

"I remember them in the locker room," Comer said. "They had a contract with them and they told me to sign it and come to Delaware State. It had been raining that day and I remember the contract was wet."

Comer was excited. "I'm signing this right now," he said to himself. Not only did he want to continue his football career, no one in his family had ever gone to college. He was so excited, in fact, that he thought Purzycki and Billings were from Delaware. He had already signed when he realized they weren't offering him a scholarship to UD, but to Delaware State. His reaction?

"I knew that they lost that 105-to-nothing game against Portland State. I thought Del State was an even better situation for me. I could go there and help put them on the map."

When the day came for Comer to leave home and go to Delaware State for football training camp, his stepfather was working and couldn't drive him to Dover. His neighbor knew where Delaware State was and offered to take him.

"He had a truck that looked like the one the Beverly Hillbillies drove. We pulled up on campus and everyone was looking at me and thinking 'this must be a country ass boy and he must be poor as hell.'"

Comer's family was actually doing OK. "My stepfather worked for the United States Postal Service as a truck driver, he had a Cadillac, we owned our home and we weren't poor."

Nevertheless, when he got out of a truck that looked like Jed Clampett's carrying all his things in a big trash bag and a suitcase, Comer was feeling more than a little self-consciousness. He tried to blunt that by showing every bit of West Philly cool he could muster as he walked towards the dormitory. He then blew any shot he had at a good entrance by walking right into a glass door that he thought was open.

The snickering that accompanied his arrival turned into full-on laughter. Comer gathered his senses, shook his head to clear the cobwebs, and turned around to go back to the truck. His mom Beverly and family had accompanied him on the trip and they had watched him walk into the door. "I don't think I want to go here," Comer told his mom. "I want to go home."

"Your ass is staying here," she replied with a mom-style firmness that indicated the discussion was over. "You're the first one in this family to go to college and you're from West Philadelphia High School. You're a tough son of a gun and you're staying at Delaware State."

Steven Holiday played in the same all-star game as Comer and also was offered a scholarship to Del State. ("We were offering on faith," Billings said. "We knew nothing about them. Nothing. We saw 'em in one game and that was it.").

Holiday remembered that during his visit to DSC that spring there was still plenty of emotion regarding Purzycki's hire. "I talked to several players who didn't speak kindly about Joe. I know it was an HBCU school, but I didn't realize the controversy about his hiring ran so deep. They kept complaining that they didn't think he knew anything about our culture and that there were more qualified black candidates who had been passed over. There were a lot of people who were afraid of change."

Holiday listened to the complaints but didn't give them much weight. Purzycki had recruited him and wanted him to come to Delaware State. All of his experiences with the new coach had been good and he didn't see any reason that would change. When he arrived for his freshman year many of the guys who had tried to talk him out of coming to play for Purzycki were gone.

"I got there, and I was like, 'Where's everybody at? What happened here?' But it was better that those guys left," he said. "You don't need that going on if you're trying to build something."

Not all of the detractors left. Frank Burton was a wide receiver from Wilmington, Delaware, who chose Del State because he wanted to play baseball in addition to football. Purzycki had no problem with that. When Burton arrived, he was surprised at how much acrimony still simmered around the new coach.

"There were still a lot of disgruntled guys who were trying to poison the team," he said. "The guys coming in had been recruited by Joe, but the guys who were already there were saying, 'This white guy is coming in and saying he's going to change us. He doesn't know our culture or how to relate to us.' There was a lot of tension and noise."

Burton says it was clear to him that he had a choice. He could try to make things work, or he could side with those who were disgruntled. And he had experience in such matters.

He had grown up in a predominantly black neighborhood in Wilmington. When he was entering high school in 1978, Delaware passed a law that mandated school busing. Instead of attending school in the city, Burton was bussed to Brandywine High School in a predominantly white neighborhood north of town.

"When we arrived at school, there was an atmosphere that no parent would want their child to experience. It was still summer, so all the windows were down on the bus and there was a group of parents standing on a sidewalk near the school holding protest signs and shouting at us, 'Niggers go home! We don't want you here!' It was visceral."

Some of the protestors threw things at Burton and his fellow black classmates as they scrambled off the bus and into their new school. Inside, things weren't much better.

"It was very volatile at first," Burton related. "They didn't want us out there and we didn't want to be there. There were a lot of fights and there was a lot of tension."

But as the black kids and white kids got to know each other the situation started to improve. People competing on all the fall sports teams began to value uniform color more than skin color.

"The athletes from the city and the suburbs came together," Burton said. "When we got on the field, we were competing against the other team and that's all that mattered. We found out their stories were our stories and our stories were their stories. Their laughs were our laughs. Their hurts were our hurts. We began to feel like we could make a change in people's attitudes and a difference in the school."

He said other students saw the camaraderie grow among black and white athletes. The growing relationships influenced others and gradually led to a willingness within the community to be more accepting of black students. Now, three years later, Burton found himself in another volatile situation based on skin color.

"At Del State, it was flipped," he said. "It wasn't white students, players, and administrators who were upset. It was the black students, players, and administrators saying just the opposite. 'We don't want a white boy in here. This guy doesn't know anything about our culture.' Since I had the experiences I had I was able to speak up and encourage teammates to give him a chance, to look past his skin color and focus on what's he saying, his vision for the program."

Burton distinctly recalls the pointed question of an upperclassman: "Hey man, are you going to be a sellout? Are you going to be an Uncle Tom?"

"Let me tell you what my theory is," Burton responded. "There are three sides to every story. There's your side, Coach Purzycki's side, and somewhere in the middle is the truth. I want to know what the truth is so I'm not listening to all this noise. I'm going to make my assessment on how I deal with Coach Purzycki based on my relationship with him. It's not going to be based on anything you say."

Still, Burton saw the other side of the story. "I could see their point because of what I had experienced when I first got to Brandywine High School."

Joe Lane said he could feel tension within the team in that first training camp, but he disregarded the naysayers for two reasons.

"For me, it wasn't a big deal because I just wanted to play football and Coach Purzycki was giving me that chance," he said, "and to be honest, I didn't even know Delaware State was an HBCU until I got into school."

Comer thinks some of the negative reaction was caused by Purzycki's implementation of rules and discipline into the program.

"A lot of the backlash came from upperclassmen who weren't used to that," he said. "Coach was very strict, and he had to earn the player's respect. To do that, he had to be tough on certain things. Some guys didn't like that."

They weren't too crazy about Comer and the new recruits, either. New coaches can hardly avoid showing a measure of favoritism to players who joined the cause in their very first recruiting class. At least some returning players are bound to harbor suspicions and complaints – it's natural in any coaching change. And it was particularly acute at Del State in the fall of 1981.

The newly arriving players were just excited to be there and had no preconceived notion of how things had unfolded. Purzycki and his staff had chosen them to help build the program, and the reciprocated loyalty of the freshmen was undeniable. At the start of training camp, Comer got a sense of the divide that existed between the veterans and the newcomers.

Tradition at Del State dictated that freshman had to wear shirts that said "Gnat" on them. They weren't true Hornets yet, not until they made it through training camp. Recruits were also supposed to have their heads shaved. Comer balked at both requests.

"My point was, I'm from the streets of Philadelphia, and we don't do that kind of stuff," he said. "I had just gotten my haircut to come to college and you think I'm going to shave it into a mohawk? I'm not doing it."

The next day at practice, Comer noticed one of the guys who had been on him to cut his hair was lined up opposite him for a drill. Comer put a move on the guy and caught a pass as Purzycki boomed, "Oh my God! Who makes a move like that? Look at that guy we recruited! Ace Comer!"

Purzycki continued to rave as Comer turned back toward the huddle and was suddenly thumped by the defender. "The guy was so pissed off that a few seconds after the play was over, he speared me right in my back."

Purzycki intervened and tossed the offender out of practice with a quick speech to the team that such behavior was not going to be tolerated.

To some returning players – those still not fully sold on the new coach – this was another afront. Purzycki's reaction to the late hit equated to babying his rookies. Again. After all, hazing was accepted as tradition in many football programs, and he had ripped it away from the upperclassmen.

"I put an end to it at Del State," Purzycki said. "I told the upper-classmen to stop messing with the young guys. We didn't have much talent, we weren't very good, and I didn't want people quitting the team and leaving us for something as pointless as hazing."

For his part, Comer was pegged as "Purzycki's son" by his teammates.

But it was becoming clear that there were plenty of guys who had bought in. They were there to play football, wanted things to improve, and recognized that Purzycki and his staff really had a plan. They noticed more structure in the practice sessions and a higher level of personal accountability.

"At one of our first practices," tight end Terry Staples said, "I missed a block and Coach Billings got all in my face and told me he was embarrassed. I didn't like it, but the next time the player in front of me was in trouble."

"They didn't allow us to just gloss over mistakes," quarterback Sam Warren said. "I remember Joe every day at practice walking around yelling 'Coaches! You've gotta do some teaching out here.'"

Thunder Thornton had played eight different positions (for several different coaches) in his career at Del State. For his senior year, he was going to be a defensive end. That meant he worked for new defensive coordinator Bill Collick.

"I remember he was almost impossible to please," he said. "He had very high standards and was always demanding more. That made me better, so I liked it."

"Collick was the type who could just look at you and get you to do your best," Anthony Sharpe said. "He wasn't a yeller or a screamer. Coaches can command respect in different ways."

Collick's contributions ran deeper than just what he taught on the field. Players watched him and saw a black man not much older than them talking and laughing and interacting with Purzycki and Billings on a daily basis. He became someone players went to if they had big-picture questions about the situation.

"Bill kept us together," said Walt Samuels. "He was a dude of wisdom and a lot of people gravitated to him. I talked to him often when I was there. He was no-nonsense, he didn't play, and people respected that in him. When you talked to him, you knew that he knew what he was talking about. He was sage."

Collick knew that there were limited opportunities for black head coaches, but he would remind players who didn't like the idea of a white head coach at an HBCU that Delaware State had been a leader in integration both with students and faculty.

"We may have come in different ships, but we're in the same boat now," he'd tell them, using one of his favorite quotes of Dr. Martin Luther King.

He'd tell players about his Uncle Carl who had graduated from Delaware State in the 1940s (when it was still called the State College for Colored Students). Carl Collick had an interest in chemistry and was befriended by a teacher named George Seidel who put him on a path to become a chemist. Carl Collick ended up having a successful 35-year career with the City of Philadelphia Navy Yard.

"This was a time when opportunities like that were not common for a young black man," Collick would say. "Do you think it mattered to my uncle that Dr. Seidel was white? Of course not."

Collick would listen to the player's questions about Purzycki, football, and life. To anyone who was considering leaving he'd bring it back to his overriding belief that the three most important things in life were education, education, and education. He often told players, "A college degree can get you in the door in places where you might not have been able to even get in the neighborhood."

The staff was full of fiery guys, but offensive line coach Jeff Cannon was much more likely to make his points in a calm, measured tone. Cannon was an All-American defensive lineman at Delaware in 1973. He and Collick had known each other since they were lifeguards together during their college summers at Rehoboth Beach, Delaware.

"He cared about his players beyond football," Collick said. "You got more out of Jeff Cannon than just coaching. You got the human side of college football. We were chasing respectability and he really helped with that. He wanted to win as much as anyone else, but his attitude was, 'We're going to get better with each practice, and we're going to get better with each game, and we'll see where that leads us.' He always kept things in proper perspective."

Cannon (who died in a 1998 traffic accident) was an artist who would spend time drawing caricatures of the players and coaches designed to motivate them and/or make them laugh.

The staff was rounded out by receivers coach Walt Tullis, who had helped Purzycki connect with players in the spring, and Greg McLaurin, who coached the defensive backs. Tullis was from Hartford, Connecticut, and had played for DSC. McLaurin was from Wilmington, Delaware, and had played college ball at nearby Salisbury State.

McLaurin said Tullis was a key to changing what had been a lackadaisical culture around football at Delaware State.

"The players told us that before we arrived, it was almost like a rec league attitude," McLaurin said. "Sometimes guys would come to practice, sometimes they wouldn't. Guys would miss here and there, and we didn't tolerate that. Walt helped us because of his experience in pro football. He stressed the consistency necessary to play at the top level."

"You go to weight room sessions," Tullis told the players. "You go to meetings, and you go to practice. On time. All the time."

They added two part-time coaches, John Covaleski, who was the former JV coach at Caesar Rodney High School, and Robbie Schroeder who was a friend of Collick's from childhood days.

One of Purzycki's goals for sustained success at Del State was to give the program more of a local feel. His first staff certainly did that. Of his seven assistants, five were from Delaware. He and Tullis were the only non-Delawareans but they had both played college ball in the First State.

The staff brought youth, enthusiasm, and football knowledge to the team. The new players loved it and even some of the veterans who had been unsure about Purzycki had to admit that the staff as a whole was an upgrade over the previous year. Things were organized, practices were positive, and improvement was obvious.

"By the time training camp ended," Burton said, "the people who were paying attention and could discern such things could tell that

Coach Purzycki and his staff had vision. It wasn't just talk. There was a whole lot of action. Joe knew the odds were against him during the entire transition period, but he was confident, he had vision ... and I liked his tenacity."

SIXTEEN

Rookie college head football coach Joe Purzycki walked onto the field at State College Stadium in Orangeburg, South Carolina, and headed for the Delaware State sideline. It was about an hour until kickoff and the Hornets were stretching and warming up for their game against South Carolina State University.

Delaware State (loser of nine games by an average of nearly 40 points per game in 1980) opened the 1981 season one week earlier in Petersburg, Virginia, and played Virginia State tough. They lost, 13-12, but had the ball deep in VSU territory when the Trojans stopped them on fourth-and-one. "I messed up an assignment on that play and probably cost us the game," said offensive tackle Franz Kappel.

A freshman, Kappel started and played the entire game. He was a good example of the type of player who found himself in Purzycki's first recruiting class. Delaware State was the last place he ever thought he'd be.

Kappel was a star player at William Penn High School in New Castle and had gotten a lot of attention from major Division I schools. But an injury his sophomore year left him unable to bend his knee more than 90 degrees. Big schools loved his talent but were scared off when they saw his knee. "I wouldn't have recruited me," Kappel said.

In his mad scramble to find players, Purzycki ignored the knee issue and saw only talent that he desperately needed.

"Desperate is a good word," Kappel said. "He was throwing scholarships to anyone who would say 'hi' to him. My high school coach called a few of us into the office and Purzycki gave us his spiel. He concluded by saying 'If any of you are interested, there's a scholarship waiting for you."

Kappel's reaction? "I just giggled. I told him he was nuts if he thought I was going to Del State." As the weeks went by and the big schools who had been interested kept backing away, Kappel saw the writing on the wall and reconsidered. He had two offers: one from Ferrum Junior College with no money, and one from Delaware State with a full scholarship. He called Purzycki and said he'd had a change of heart.

Purzycki loved Kappel's attitude and talent. His blown assignment at the end of the VSU game had been costly, but one play doesn't determine a game's outcome. The coach saw nothing but potential in the young man who had laughed in his face when he originally asked him to play at Del State.

Virginia State was a road game but close enough to Dover that the Hornets traveled and played on the same day. Game two at South Carolina State was almost 600 miles away. Purzycki checked itineraries from his days at Delaware to see how the Blue Hens handled similar trips, and then he spoke to Townsend.

"I want the team to leave Thursday morning," he told the AD. "We'll bus to Orangeburg, check into the hotel Thursday night, practice Friday, play Saturday, then come home."

Townsend smiled and told Purzycki that he and the team could leave on Thursday, but not until almost midnight. "That way," he said, "the players can sleep overnight on the bus, which saves us money. You'll get there on Friday at noon, have your practice, then check into the hotel." It was another reminder to the coach that he wasn't at Delaware anymore. Delaware State's team bus was an old, past-its-prime coach that the players had long ago nicknamed the "Gray Ghost."

"It had a bathroom," Thunder Thornton related, "but there was nothing about it that was luxurious."

Thursday night came and Purzycki was impressed that his players, particularly the veterans, arrived at the bus well before the planned departure time. He wanted his team to be on time, which (like most coaches) meant early. If the upperclassmen on the squad were buying into this idea, he was making progress.

He soon realized that their prompt arrival wasn't an effort to please the new coach.

"The guys who had made this kind of trip before got on the bus as soon as it arrived and started jumping onto the luggage racks above the seats," he laughed. "They weren't trying to impress me, they just wanted to get the best spots for sleeping on an overnight bus trip."

When the luggage racks filled up, players claimed spots in the aisle. The last to arrive (along with the coaching staff) would sleep sitting up. Nocturnal travel wasn't unique to Delaware State. Most HBCU football teams made similar arrangements for lengthy trips. Limited budgets meant limited accommodations.

It had been tough for Purzycki to get a foothold in Dover but at least he was there every day and could sense some progress. Road games were a different story. Townsend had warned him that he'd likely face some antagonism from players, coaches, and fans of other teams who felt his hiring as a slap in the face. Townsend wanted Purzycki to be aware of what he was walking into, and in the case of Orangeburg, that was a college town with deep racial scars.

On February 8, 1968, South Carolina State University was the site of a rally protesting segregation. As tensions escalated between students and police, a policeman fired his gun into the air, apparently attempting to restore order. Other officers upon hearing the shot, fired into the crowd. Three students, all teenagers, were killed, and 27 were wounded. An investigation concluded that most of the wounded were shot in the back as they fled.

In the wake of the shootings, nine officers were brought to trial. All nine were acquitted. Thirteen years after the "Orangeburg Massacre" many people in the SCSU community remained resentful, and a high level of mistrust persisted. This was a place with especially jagged emotions, and the very idea that a black college football team was being coached by a white man remained troublesome.

"You're heading into the old south," Townsend told him. "It's still segregated and if there's anywhere you're going to face difficulties, this might be the place."

Purzycki already knew how SCSU coach Bill Davis felt. At the pre-season MEAC coaches meeting, Davis had been among those who refused to speak to him. He let others know that he hated the idea of Purzycki being the head coach at Del State. (On this day he would forego the traditional pregame meeting between head coaches as well.)

Purzycki let his assistants handle stretching and warmups. As they walked through the lines of players, giving encouragement and reminders, he took a seat on the Hornets' bench to go over his notes and focus on what he was going to say to his team before kickoff.

They faced a tall task. South Carolina State was coming off a 10-and-1 season and this game would be the Bulldogs' 1981 home opener. They were a true HBCU dynasty. Few schools their size had produced one Pro Football Hall of Famer, but SCSU had three: Harry Carson, Deacon Jones, and Marion Motley. The place dripped with football success and history.

The Bulldogs were favored to win the MEAC and would likely have no trouble with Del State and their new coach. As Purzycki sat on the bench, one of the South Carolina State assistant coaches made his way over to the Del State sideline. Just within earshot of Purzycki, he began talking.

"Look at this, fellas." he addressed his players. "The white man is over here sitting down while the black man is working."

"He was a big defensive line coach and he was just jaw-jacking, trying to intimidate us," said secondary coach Greg McLaurin.

It took Purzycki a moment to process what he had heard. In case he missed it, the coach repeated himself. "White man sitting while the black man is working," he said coldly. "Some things never change."

Purzycki definitely heard him the second time and instinctively jumped off the bench to find something to do. McLaurin intervened. "Hey!" he yelled at the SCSU coach. "We don't need any of that kind of talk. Knock it off! Get away from our sideline."

"Oh, sorry," the coach responded. "What's the massuh got you doing today?" McLaurin and the coach verbally sparred for another minute ("I was giving him just as much back as I was getting.") before the SCSU assistant retreated, pleased that he'd struck a nerve.

"We're here," McLaurin yelled as he launched a parting shot. "We're not going anywhere." South Carolina State won 29-0.

On the long trip home from the game, his second loss in as many games, Purzycki recalled Townsend's statement during their very first meeting about the black college football community: *There are people who are not going to be happy with a white man taking a leadership position at Delaware State College."*

For months, Purzycki told everyone who asked that he just wanted to be a football coach. But it was finally sinking in that he was more than that. He was, as one sportswriter described him, "a social experiment."

That week, Purzycki spoke to the Del State booster club at a luncheon. A master storyteller, he was at home in front of a crowd and knew the value of self-deprecating humor. The September 1981 issue of *Delaware Today Magazine* featured a cover photo of Purzycki with the headline "Is This the Dick Vermeil of Delaware?" Purzycki was 0-and-2 since the cover story had come out.

"My wife Sharon told me *Delaware Today Magazine* wants to put me on the cover again in October," he told the boosters. "This time, it's just going to say 'NO!'"

The coach knew he was staring 0-and-3 in the face. If there was any team in the MEAC tougher than South Carolina State it was Florida A&M. The Rattlers were a powerhouse in HBCU football and the home team figured on an easy win over Del State.

Similar to the week before in South Carolina, Purzycki heard some ugly barbs from fans as he walked onto the field. "Some of the fans at those games were yelling racial epithets at him," said Matt Horace. "It made us angry because to us he represented positive things."

"It felt like South Carolina State and Florida A&M looked down upon us because they were so much better than us," Mike Colbert said. "And now, we had a white coach, and they looked down on us because of that."

Alabama coach Bear Bryant long ago had begun a tradition of being escorted on the field by a pair of Alabama state police officers. If it was good for the Bear, it was good for others. So, throughout the South, coaches often were accompanied by state troopers – complete with double-brimmed Smokey the Bear-style hats – as a symbol of strength.

Rattlers' coach Rudy Hubbard was no different and was flanked by a pair of Florida lawmen as Purzycki approached to shake hands.

Mindful of the earful of hate he had received from fans as he walked into the stadium, he laughed nervously as he reached

Hubbard and gestured towards the two officers. "Hi Coach," Purzycki said. "You know, I think I might need those guys more than you do."

Hubbard was another guy who had been chilly to him at the MEAC coaches pre-season gathering, and as Purzycki's pre-game attempt to break the ice, the Florida A&M coach made sure the joke fell flat – he just stood there, staring at him. The Rattlers won 27-3.

The following week the Hornets finally played a home game and held a 16-6 lead over West Chester State before the Golden Rams scored two touchdowns in the final five minutes to win the game.

"I feel like my patron saint has abandoned me right now," Purzycki told reporters after the game. "St. Jude is the patron saint of impossible causes and he picked up and left me today."

The team was winless but the players, particularly the veterans, were seeing progress. Purzycki and his staff weren't yet winning but the team was already showing significant improvement.

Nigel Dunn was a versatile offensive lineman who played high school football in Miami, Florida, for a team that lost a total of five games while he was there. He had seen what it takes to be successful in football and by the end of the 1980 Del State season knew things had to change. He had played for white coaches in high school so Purzycki's skin color meant nothing to him.

"As soon as he started I knew it was going to be different," Dunn said. "I could see Purzycki had great organization skills. It was a lot of little things but the difference from years past was night and day. How you dressed for road trips, itineraries, a consistent practice schedule, making sure we kept the locker room clean; a lot of little things that help a team win. He gave us discipline that year that became the foundation for our success."

The previous coaching staff often dealt with mistakes on the field by dialing up the level of contact and intensity on the practice field in a misguided effort to make players tougher. That changed in 1981.

"Joe never did anything that was punitive," Horace said. "He never stopped practice and made us run for an hour as a punishment. He knew there was nothing productive about that. Under Coach Henderson, we were always tired. Sometimes you could barely walk after practice you'd hurt so much."

The attention to discipline extended to how Purzycki interacted with his staff.

"Joe spent a lot of time making sure that we knew what we were doing," Collick said. "He'd constantly grill you about the offense, the defense, and the players to make sure we were all on the same page. His attention to detail was important and never more than in that first fall."

All that said, there's a big scoreboard at one end of a football field for a reason. And as 0-and-4 turned to 0-and-5 after a home loss to conference foe Bethune Cookman, everyone was beginning to feel some heat.

"Doesn't matter if it's high school fans on Saturday morning or college fans on Sunday morning," Collick said with a laugh, "If you ain't got a half point more than the other team someone's looking at you funny."

Purzycki continually reminded himself and his staff that theirs was a long-term mission that would likely include many setbacks along the way. But they needed a win. For the players. For themselves. And for Nelson Townsend, who was getting a steady stream of complaints about his winless new head football coach.

Joe Purzycki at his first press conference.
"I just want to coach football."

Nelson Townsend. *"I don't care if Purzycki is purple, or from Mars. He is the guy I want leading this program."*

Bill Collick. *"He was a dude of wisdom. He was sage."*

Herky Billings (right). *"He was the kind of guy who made the game fun."*

Delaware State president Dr. Luna Mishoe.
"He didn't agree with the decision (to hire Purzycki), but he supported Townsend and allowed him to see his vision through."

Purzycki on the sideline.
"I never met anyone in coaching or business who motivated me more."

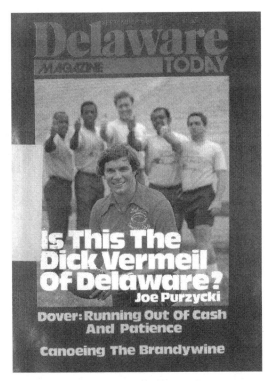

Purzycki with his staff in 1981. Greg McLaurin, Walt Tullis, Jeff Cannon, Bill Collick, and Herky Billings (l to r).

The Hornets watch as offensive line coach Jeff Cannon diagrams a play.

JOSEPH R. BIDEN, JR.
DELAWARE

6021 FEDERAL BUILDING
844 KING STREET
WILMINGTON, DELAWARE 19801
(302) 573-6345

United States Senate
WASHINGTON, D.C. 20510

October 21, 1981

The Delaware State College Football Team
c/o Mr. Joseph Purzycki
Head Coach
Delaware State College
Athletic Department
Dover, Delaware   19901

Dear Team Members,

I've been following your season and was really moved by the articles written about you --- especially the one this past Sunday that reported how a 1-and-6 football team displayed so much positive and enthusiastic emotion.

While I usually find myself writing letters to teams that win championships, I felt I had to write and let you know that I think you guys are something special.

The heart-breaking losses that you suffered would have broken many teams. You not only have stuck together, but seem to have improved your on-the-field performance, game by game.

It is this kind of team effort upon which winning traditions are built.

Keep that winning attitude. Keep building your confidence. And, if you want it badly enough, you can win your last 4 games -- then next year, the conference championship!

Congratulations, and keep up the good work.

Sincerely,

Joseph R. Biden, Jr.
United States Senator

Delaware State's first win under Purzycki caught the eye of a
United States senator.

Purzycki's hiring brought Delaware State football national attention.

Halfback Steve Holiday.
"Mr. Townsend hired the best man for the job and in a lot of cases back then, and still today, people in positions of power don't do that."

Andre Williams and Gary Hicks celebrate a Hornets win.

Gene Lake set several Delaware State records after coaches
discovered him at a flag football game.

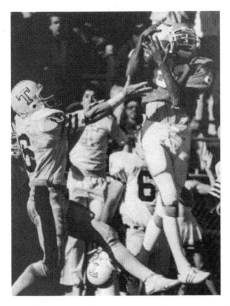

At first, everyone thought the new guy was named Jake. By the
time he was done rewriting the Delaware State record book, they
all knew who John Taylor was.

John Taylor had 150 yards receiving and four touchdowns in this game in 1983 when he outdueled another future NFL star, Gary Clark of James Madison.

Defensive lineman Joe Lane.
"Purzycki knew how to talk to us. The way he quoted Dr. King and others, you could tell it was coming from a place in his heart."

Delaware State breaks into Top 20

By ED MURPHY
Staff reporter

DOVER — Delaware State College has finally received national football recognition.

DelState, which has won five straight games, broke into the NCAA Division I-AA Top 20 poll at the No.15 position Monday.

The Hornets, who have produced three teams with winning records over the past 20 years, are ranked for the first time. DelState is 2-1 in the Mid-Eastern Athletic Conference and 5-1 overall.

"I just heard about it one minute ago," Hornet Coach Joe Purzycki said from his office after hearing the good news Monday afternoon. "I tell you, for all the things we have had to do to build the program, it is very important to get this kind of recognition.

It has been quite a turnaround for a football program that lost 105-0 to Portland State and finished 2-9 in 1980. Since taking over the helm in 1981, Purzycki has revived the dying Hornet football program.

But the Hornets have made great strides in the MEAC and Division I-AA standings this year.

DelState was looked over in the I-AA poll last week, but its impressive 26-7 win over North Carolina A&T Saturday helped vault the Hornets into the limelight.

"We are just as pleased as anything that the committee has recognized the consistancy of our performances," said Purzycki. "The MEAC has been in Division I-AA for three or four years. I don't believe you will find a Hornet team that has been ranked on any poll in the last 20 years.

"It is very prestigious and a shot in the arm for all of us. From our mode of thinking, we have to maintain our consistancy to stay in the rankings."

DelState missed being ranked in the Top 20 by one point after upsetting James Madison University 38-28 two weeks ago. The Hornets

Division I-AA Top 20

MISSION, Kan. (AP) — The Top 20 teams in the National Collegiate Athletic Association Division I-AA football poll, with this season's records and points:

#	Team	Record	Points
1.	Eastern Kentucky	5-0-0	80
2.	Southern Illinois	7-0-0	75
3.	Jackson State	7-0-0	71
4.	Holy Cross	6-0-0	70
5.	S.C. State	6-1-0	63
6.	Northeast La.	5-1-0	57
7.	North Texas State	5-2-0	52
8.	Furman	4-1-1	47
9.	Eastern Ill.	6-1-0	45
(tie)	Idaho State	5-1-0	45
11.	Middle Tenn.	5-1-0	43
12.	Tennessee State	4-1-1	42
13.	Colgate	4-2-0	30
14.	Indiana State	5-2-0	28
15.	Delaware State	5-1-0	22
16.	Nevada-Reno	3-3-0	19
17.	Weber State	5-1-0	12
18.	McNeese State	4-2-0	10
(tie)	Southern, La.	5-1-0	10
20.	Boston U.	4-2-0	7

were impressive with in their easy win over the Aggies Saturday.

The four-man committee, which voted for the Hornets, consists of Andrew Moordian of New Hampshire, Edward Teague of The Citadel, Donald Combs of Eastern Kentucky and Idaho State's I.J. Caccia. All voted for the Hornets Monday.

"Delaware State was so close last week and when you continue to win like they have, it's possible to make a pretty big jump in the ratings," Jerry Miles, the director of men's championships for the NCAA said Monday.

Losses by Lafayette (17th) and Idaho (19th), and a tie by Grambling (20th), helped the Hornets chances. DelState, which lost to fifth-ranked South Carolina State in the first game of the season, bumped those three and Appalachian State, N.C.

"I was talking to the AD (Athletic Director Nelson Townsend) and we discussed what this means to us," Purzycki said. "It is a feather in our cap."

October 1983. *"Nelson! You have GOT to see this!"*

116

SEVENTEEN

The Hornets' sixth consecutive loss that season came in a gut-wrenching four-point setback to Howard.

Hard as it was to lose a close game, it was even more difficult for Purzycki and his team because they all felt that the game had turned on a call that went against them late in the third quarter. When quarterback Pat Spencer hit wide receiver Walt Samuels on a pass over the middle, Samuels fought his way into the end zone. But as he crossed the goal line, he lost the football. Officials quickly ruled it a fumble, no TD, Howard ball.

Purzycki and his players exploded in anger. In every game, at what always felt like key moments, a big call would go against them.

"I remember a couple of calls going against us that shouldn't have," said lineman Matt Horace, "and I remember the officials smirking as Purzycki was turning red and going crazy on the sidelines. That's when I first understood that coach was facing some real hate. There was a lot of consternation around the league because people thought if he had success other black coaches were going to lose their jobs."

After the Howard game, Samuels was asked about the play. "I was over the goal line, I'm sure of that," he snapped at *News Journal* reporter Jack Ireland. At least Samuels stayed long enough to snap at someone. Purzycki, for the only time in his career, left the stadium without talking to reporters. He knew it looked bad, but his frustration got the better of him. Townsend met with Purzycki a day or two after every game. Their conversation after the Howard game began with Townsend stating the obvious.

"You've got to talk to the reporters after the game," Townsend said. "That's part of your job."

"What am I going to say?" Purzycki responded. "I'm getting hosed every week. *We're* getting hosed. Am I going to complain that I think we're not getting calls because I'm white?"

"Here's how it works in the black community," Townsend said. "This happens to us all the time. Everything we go into; the deck is stacked against us. You either get mad, or you find a way. You're going to have to find a way to be at least a touchdown better than good because you're not going to get a lot of breaks."

That didn't make it fair or right, but Townsend felt that in his life when it came to getting an education, getting a job, and even hiring a white man to coach at an HBCU, unfairness was a common obstacle. Purzycki would have to learn to deal with it and still come out ahead.

Purzycki appreciated that Townsend agreed that some of the dubious penalty flags had the feel of something more than just bad calls. He knew that not talking to the media after a loss was a bad idea; it did not present a positive image for him, the football team, and the school. A few days later he tried to explain himself to the *State News*.

"Being an emotional person to start with, and then going through that frustration, I was very upset," he said. "When you lose your fourth game by a touchdown or less, your frustration comes out in anger and all kinds of other ways. The bad calls are happening every week. We're catching enough flags that anyone would get frustrated."

Meanwhile, Townsend was hearing about the 0-and-6 start from just about everyone. School president Luna Mishoe would good-naturedly kid him in private (and occasionally in front of others). "*Your* coach hasn't won a game yet," he'd say to Townsend. "*Your* coach is 0-and-6. *Your* coach didn't too well last week."

Townsend took the shots with a thin smile. Mishoe had been clear with him from the start on this matter.

"Dr. Mishoe wasn't in agreement with hiring Purzycki," said Diane Townsend. "He never came down on Nelson personally, but he'd always say to him, 'Man, I hope you know what you're doing.'"

Townsend understood the situation. Mishoe had people above him who weren't keen on the hiring and he had to manage their expectations. These people provided money and support to the school and Mishoe would occasionally indicate to them privately that he had not been in favor of the hire. His style was to let people make decisions and then hold them accountable and that's what he planned to do in this case. At times, Townsend was disappointed with how Mishoe reacted, but he understood.

"I can't be angry with him because he has to report to other people," he once told Diane. "It's not just me he has to be concerned with."

"That's why he was able to tolerate it," Diane Townsend said. "Mishoe had to play a game. He was a good president, but he made it clear that if Purzycki wasn't successful, it was going to be on Nelson."

Your coach.

Townsend also was getting a steady stream of phone calls at home in the evenings from people who supported the team but still questioned the hiring of Purzycki. He could see the improvement in the team across the board from what he saw on that rainy, rotten night in Portland. Nevertheless, 0-and-6 is 0-and-6.

"He had a lot of phone calls," Diane Townsend said. "He would talk to them and explain why he had hired Joe. He'd explain that he thought the best way for Delaware State to get good at football was to try to do things the way they were done at Delaware."

By the time Townsend was done, according to his wife, he usually had won over the person on the other end of the line. But only to a point.

"People would understand better after talking to him why he had picked Purzycki. They'd tell him 'I see what you're saying, but I can't go outside and talk that way around my friends and support that idea.' The people they were friends with, the people they talked to and went to games with, they couldn't say to them that they thought Joe was a good idea."

So, when Purzycki's name came up on campus, at the games, and around town, opinions had already been formed against the new coach. And that 0-and-6 start solidified those opinions as virtually unanimous.

Townsend was firm in his support but often told Diane that two games concerned him. North Carolina A&T and Central State College. The two coaches who had been in competition with Purzycki for the Del State job were Jim McKinley, who had stayed at NC A&T, and Billy Joe, who had been hired by Central State after being passed over by Del State.

"All he has to do the first year is win those two games," Townsend said. "Beat McKinley and beat Joe. That's it."

The following Saturday, it appeared Purzycki was going to whiff on the first half of that assignment. McKinley's Aggies had just scored a nail-in-the-coffin touchdown to take a 17-6 lead with 3:37 left in the game. The Townsends sat among the agitated crowd at Alumni Stadium. Occasionally, a voice could be heard making disparaging remarks about the soon to be 0-and-7 coach and the AD who had hired him.

But suddenly, the Hornets Wing-T offense came to life. They drove the length of the field and when Johnny Rowe dragged three defenders into the end zone for a touchdown, the deficit was 17-12. Then quarterback Spencer dashed in for the two-point conversion, and with 2:13 remaining in the game, only a field goal separated the teams.

On the Del State sideline, Purzycki considered an onside kick but since they had all three of their timeouts, he decided to kick deep. The message was clear: if the DSC defense could stop them, the Hornets offense would finish the job.

The defense did their part, delivering a three-and-out. The Hornets got the ball back on their own 26 and quickly marched downfield again. Spencer hit Samuels for 16 yards and 11 yards. Rowe had runs of 30 yards and 12. Spencer ran the final three yards into the end zone with 43 seconds remaining and when Bobby Swoope added the extra point the Hornets had shockingly taken a 21-17 lead.

The Aggies didn't go quietly, reaching the DSC 14 before the last play of the game, a pass into the end zone that fell incomplete. Final from Dover: Del St 21, NC A&T 17.

The Hornets offense rushed onto the field and mobbed the defense. Players hugged and danced in what Jack Ireland called "an emotional outburst that resembled the reaction of a team that had just won a national championship."

Purzycki hurriedly found McKinley and the two shook hands. While many people had treated his arrival at Del State and the MEAC with disdain, McKinley had been warm and welcoming. At the MEAC coaches' preseason meeting, when some wouldn't even speak to Purzycki, McKinley invited him to his home for dinner. "One of the most gracious things that ever happened to me," Purzycki said. "I never forgot that gesture of friendship."

He turned to run over and join his team, but that journey was interrupted by his athletic director who had run across the field to greet *his* victorious coach. Townsend picked Purzycki up off the ground and squeezed him in a bear hug. "I'm proud of you, Joe. Great job!"

By this point, the players determined that Purzycki wouldn't need his legs to get back to the locker room.

"I had never been a part of carrying someone off the field," Thunder Thornton said. "We had lost so many close games and to finally get one, we were so pumped up. A whole bunch of us just surrounded him and picked him up."

"In your life as a coach, it's a rare thing to get carried off the field," he said. "It's exhilarating. I'm 0-and-6, and I've taken a lot of crap and so have the players. There are people on campus telling them 'Don't play for this guy.' There are guys in the locker room not buying in and sowing seeds of discontent. And we win one game and they carried me off the field. You talk about an expression of love and support."

Inside the Hornets' locker room, the celebration continued.

"I know you have listened to me for a long time and I realize some people thought our string had run out and other people even thought this team was dead," Purzycki shouted to his still revved-up team. "But I think these people are going to find out that I believe in you. I may go on to coach many different teams in my lifetime to many wins, but it will never be said that I ever felt more than I do right now for a great bunch of people. This is a special day for me, and for every one of you."

Senior defensive back Tim King, one of a small group of upperclassmen who had decided to stick with Purzycki when 17 players abandoned ship in the spring, presented the game ball to the coach.

"Guys," he told his team as he held the ball. "I'm the happiest 1-and-6 coach in the country!"

Rowe, who had racked up 149 yards on just 19 carries, was the focus of postgame media attention. A seemingly innocuous quote from him showed how things were changing for Delaware State. Rowe was a junior running back from Florida who was on his way to being the first 1,000-yard rusher in Delaware State history. He was asked about his touchdown run in the fourth quarter when he carried the three would-be tacklers into the end zone.

"I've been working on the squat lift in the weight room and can lift 300 pounds now," he said. "They were pushing me towards the sideline, but I just kept driving towards the goal line."

Two years ago, the Hornets stored what few weights they had in the weeds under the stadium. Now, thanks to an aggressive young coach and the AD who hired him, they had their own weight room and a coach who mapped out plans for them on how to use it. To hear Rowe tell it, that room had just paid a big dividend.

The room they were all celebrating in was a big deal, too. Remember, when Purzycki arrived, the locker room didn't have lockers. Players often just left games or practice in full uniform and walked back to their dorms to clean up. When he was hired, Purzycki told Townsend that a real team needed a real locker room. Townsend agreed but counseled patience while he looked for money.

Purzycki eventually grew impatient and talked to his brother Mike's father-in-law, Ed Richitelli. He asked a few friends at his country club to help out and before long they had raised the $6,000 needed to bring the Hornets' locker room up to par. It was an unanticipated benefit to hiring the new coach that there were people in the area who might never have given Delaware State football a thought, but they liked Purzycki and wanted him to succeed.

"Nelson was upset with me about that because I didn't go through proper channels to get the money," Purzycki said. "He was right, but I had to show the players that I was trying to make things better for them. Now, they had an actual locker room with stalls and a place to put their things."

On this day, Townsend didn't much care how the locker room came to be. He was happy for the team, happy for his new coach, and relieved at the thought of a Saturday night without a slew of phone calls from upset people. There was more work to be done. But today was a day to celebrate what had been accomplished.

"Today was the biggest victory of my life," Thornton told reporters. Purzycki and Townsend no doubt agreed.

EIGHTEEN

The Hornets thought they were on their way. They had a bye the week following their emotional first victory over NC A&T, so they had extra time to enjoy it and get ready for consecutive games against Division II opponents Towson State, Salisbury State, and Central State.

Coaches never admit it, but they DO look at their upcoming schedule and speculate on what might happen. Players do, too. For Del State, such speculation was suddenly enjoyable. One win didn't make them world beaters, but they had been getting better all year and now had a thrilling win that Walt Samuels said heightened the camaraderie growing within the team.

"A lot of us had played in the Portland State game," he said. "Then we had the coaching change, the controversy on campus, and players quitting. But those of us who stayed wanted to turn things around so bad. We had been through a lot together and it felt so good to get that victory."

Purzycki suddenly thought they were playing well enough to eclipse the two wins he had predicted during his job interview. But for public consumption, he downplayed everything. "I kept telling fans and the media that we weren't overly concerned about our record because our goal was to build something for the long term."

That was an appropriate goal because, in the short term, the Hornets did some backsliding.

On homecoming weekend, they laid an egg against Towson State, losing 24-7. Purzycki was upset with how his team played and particularly mad at linebacker Troy Wing who started a fight late in the sloppy game. Purzycki took Wing into the Towson State locker room after the game to apologize. "It was awkward for everyone," he said.

Perhaps the loss lingered in Purzycki's mind or maybe he saw the next game against Salisbury State as the last, best chance to get a second win in his first season. But Franz Kappel remembers that next week as one when the Hornets lost the game during practice.

"Salisbury State was the worst week of my entire life," he said. "Joe really wanted that game and he ended up working us too hard in practice. By game day, we all had rubber legs and we had nothing to give. Everyone was jelly. Young coaches make mistakes, too."

Indeed. Del State had the ball inside the one-yard line with :18 left and trailing by six. Despite having no timeouts left, Purzycki and Billings decided to run Johnny Rowe figuring even if he didn't score, they could line up fast enough to get off another play. Rowe was stopped, and quickly set the ball on the turf as the players scrambled to run another play. As he did that, a Salisbury player casually kicked the ball a few yards from where it was to be set.

The officials claimed that it was a Del State player who kicked the ball and refused to stop the clock. By the time the ball was retrieved and set for the snap, the clock expired, and Salisbury State was the 13-7 winner.

"Why in the world would one of our players kick the ball in that situation?" Collick asked after the game. "We should have been allowed to run another play." The controversial play was a killer, but Del State also fumbled the ball four times and had 11 penalties (to just four for Salisbury) and on the short trip back to Dover everyone was left to ponder yet another winnable game that had eluded their grasp.

Purzycki took heat for his decision to run in the final seconds and his 1-and-8 record had the phone ringing again at Townsend's house while Luna Mishoe pointed out to his AD, "*Your* coach had a pretty tough game down there, didn't he?"

"I'm frustrated," Townsend told reporters. "At the beginning of the season, it was felt that if there was one team we were stronger than it was Salisbury State. People complained that we were too conservative in the game and that we should have exploded against them. But that game is not a good measure of the progress or the kind of good football we've played this season."

A road game at Central State in Ohio was up next and that meant Purzycki would be coaching against Billy Joe. Much was made of that matchup, but both men downplayed any significance the events of the past winter brought to the game.

"Right after I got the job here I saw Billy Joe at a high school all-star football game," Purzycki said, "and he wished me the best of luck."

Joe's first Central State team had gotten off to a 4-and-2 start but had lost three in a row heading into the Del State game. He told reporters that he held no ill will toward Del State or Purzycki and wanted to win simply because it was the next game on the Marauders schedule.

The coaches downplayed the personal side of things, but defensive tackle Joe Lane remembered Central State games as always having a little extra bite to them. "Every game we played against Central State it felt like the fight of your life. Coach tried to downgrade it, but you could hear it in his voice that he really wanted to beat Central State."

"I remember it felt like a rivalry game when we played them," Terry Staples said. "Billy Joe's presence always made it a very intense game."

Sometimes, fans will spend a day watching two teams battle in a shining example of how to play the game at the best possible level. This was not one of those days. At least not for the offenses.

Del State managed a total of six first downs and 147 total yards. Central State moved the ball all day but had seven turnovers. One of those was an interception that Tom Kelley returned 75 yards for a touchdown, giving Del State a 13-7 lead with five minutes left in the game.

Central State promptly drove deep into DSC territory, but the Hornets defense stopped them on fourth down. The Del State offense quickly fumbled the football back to Central State. Two plays later, Thunder Thornton recovered a Central State fumble and the Hornets offense was back in business.

A first down, maybe two, was all they needed to get the win. Mindful how good DSC's defense had been and how poor their offense had executed all game Billings made a decision that sounds as ridiculous now as it did then.

"People always ask me 'What's the best call you ever made as an offensive coordinator?'" he said. "I tell them I made three of them and they all came in that game against Central State."

He called three consecutive quarterback sneaks.

"Everyone was going crazy," he said. "Greg McLaurin kept screaming 'What are you doing, Herky?' Joe gave me a look that I knew meant I was in for it if this didn't work. But I felt our best chance to win was take the clock down as far as we could. Then, by the grace of God, our punter Bret Weber uncorks a 60-yard punt that flips the field. Turns out those were the three best calls I ever made."

Del State's Victor Heflin intercepted a desperation pass on the final play of the game and the Hornets had an improbable 13-7 triumph. Defensive lineman Anthony Sharpe approached Purzycki after the game with a big smile on his face.

"We got those two jokers for you coach," he said referring to the wins over McKinley and Joe. Purzycki laughed and then thought about it aboard the Gray Ghost on the long trip back to Dover.

He still had players who didn't believe in what he was trying to do. There was still some pushback from guys on the team who weren't sure a white man should be coaching Del State. There were still people on campus filling his players' heads with reasons they shouldn't trust their new coach.

But it was obvious he had more guys with him by this point. Sharpe's comment showed an awareness and sensitivity that players were aware of the pressure on Purzycki (*and* Townsend). They now had the same number of wins as the 1980 team, but that's where any comparison ended.

"It was different," said Terry Staples. "We weren't losing by 50 or 60 points. We were losing games because of one or two mistakes. We weren't happy about 2-and-8, but the way we played gave us confidence."

They would need all that confidence against a powerful Eastern Illinois University team. EIU was a former moribund football program now enjoying the kind of success Purzycki dreamed of bringing to Dover. Between 1952 and 1977 the Panthers had exactly one winning season in 25 years. The school's administration considered eliminating the program but instead decided to hire Darrell Mudra. The team immediately started winning, as the coach lived up to his delightful nickname of "Dr. Victory."

Mudra was a genuine character. He had a Ph.D. in education and believed the authoritarian style favored by most coaches wasn't the best way to get results. He instead favored a collaborative effort that allowed his assistants room to make their own decisions. To encourage that, Dr. Victory coached games from the press box.

After successful head coaching stints at Adams State, North Dakota State, Arizona, and Western Illinois, he was named head coach at Florida State University in 1974. Tallahassee became his personal Waterloo and he was fired after winning just four game in two seasons. He was succeeded by Bobby Bowden.

Three years later EIU coaxed him back to the sideline and he delivered one of the greatest turnarounds in college football history. In 1977, the Panthers were 1-and-10. In 1978, under Mudra, they went 12-and-2 and won the Division II National Championship. His offensive coordinator that season was 26-year-old Mike Shanahan, who would go on to a become a two-time Super Bowl winning coach with the Denver Broncos. The Panthers won the championship game over Delaware, 10-9. Purzycki had been a first-year collegiate assistant on that Blue Hens team.

Eastern Illinois University is convenient from nowhere. Delaware State flew to Chicago, then to Champaign/Urbana, and then took an hour-long bus ride just to get to the game.

Sleet, wind, and cold temperatures greeted their arrival on Friday afternoon.

"It was spitting snow all weekend," according to Billings.

The Hornets did a quick run-through practice in the miserable conditions and then re-boarded the buses for the trip to their hotel.

On that ride, something happened that made Purzycki worry that a lot of what they had gained in his first season might be rubbed out. Senior guard Herb Delaney approached his coach as he got on the bus with what he thought was a funny thought.

"Coach," Delaney said, "This reminds me of the Portland State trip. It's the same setting. We're going way out to play this really good team. The weather is terrible. I sure hope we don't get beat 105-to-0."

Delaney walked off laughing but his statement stuck in Purzycki's mind like an unwanted relative who won't leave a family holiday party. He heard the words repeatedly through a restless night's sleep and climbed out of bed the next morning exhausted and nervous.

"Tubby Raymond used to say all the time," Purzycki said, "that the only thing a coach really fears is humiliation." If Delaney was right, that could be his fate today, and if the Hornets got destroyed by the bigger, faster, better Panthers the eyewitnesses would include Luna Mishoe and Nelson Townsend who were on the trip.

He knew his team had given him everything this season, but he also knew they were beaten up and barely holding it together. They were running on dwindling supplies of guts, pride, and adrenaline and were facing a superior opponent on the road. His pregame speech was designed to pull every remaining bit of energy out of his team, his coaches, and himself.

"For all we've done," he concluded after several minutes of emotional fire, "we are going to leave this season on a high note. We are NOT taking a step backward today. We will NOT let that happen. Maybe no one else can see it, but we are improving every week. We're getting better and better and that does NOT stop today!"

The Hornets charged out of the locker room onto the field to be greeted by more lousy weather and a home team that was huddled together, jumping up and down and chanting ominously: "Fifty points! Five hundred yards! Fifty points! Five hundred yards!"

Purzycki watched the Panthers as they yelled and danced and finally turned to Herky Billings with a nervous grin. "You think they might be a bit overconfident?"

Turns out, they were.

"We played our asses off that day," Purzycki said. "We were down 24-to-nothing in the fourth quarter and Johnny Rowe broke a kick return 89 yards for a touchdown. We made a two-point conversion, stopped them, Rowe had a long run for another TD, we made another two-point play and suddenly it's 24-to-16. I looked over at their players and they had eyes like saucers. I'm thinking, 'Hey! What happened to 50 points and 500 yards?'"

The final score was 24-16, and when Mudra came down from the press box and across the field to shake Purzycki's hand, he said, "Sorry, Coach. Things got a little sloppy there at the end."

Purzycki was gracious in defeat but admitted, "I wanted to say, 'Riiight. It got a little sloppy at the end. No. No. WE almost beat your ass.'"

Despite the loss, the Hornets celebrated in their locker room like winners. "That's a big-league operation over there," Purzycki told the *News Journal,* referring to EIU football. "Being competitive with them helps our kids believe in themselves. We've got 16 of our 22 starters back next year and that makes me think things are only going to get better."

Rowe finished the day with 142 yards which gave him 1,039 yards rushing on the year. He was the first guy in Delaware State College football history to top 1,000 yards rushing in a single season.

The difference in how they played and the difference in how the players felt about how they played was incalculable and important.

"Being competitive mattered not only to the players, it also mattered to the administration," Horace said. "There was so much controversy about Coach Purzycki being there that he needed to show results. If you go 2-and-9 one year, and you're getting blown out, and you don't even score a touchdown in four games ... and the next season you have the same record, but you get beat by less than a touchdown in six games, that's a measurable advance."

"My mom could tell the difference in my voice when I called home after games in 1981," said Anthony Sharpe. "She said that in 1980 I always sounded depressed. But in 1981 I felt good about how we were playing."

"Purzycki talked all season about how we were setting the foundation for others to follow," Calvin Mason said. "He told us that when we were gone people were going to be able to see what we had done. And by the end of my senior season, we were on an upswing. There had been times in prior years where we stepped on the football field and we looked pitiful. But now, you could see improvement in every game."

It had been 378 days since the morning after the Portland State debacle. At the Portland airport that day, Horace, Sharpe, Mason, and the rest of the team kept their eyes down and didn't engage anyone in small talk. Townsend had feigned disbelief when told about the game by a stranger rather than admit he was Delaware State's athletic director.

Now, no one was embarrassed to be a Del State Hornet. "We weren't pushovers anymore," Billings said. "Now, when teams played us, they knew they had been in a football game."

NINETEEN

"**H**ey, did you hear the news? 'Sweet Feet' is coming back!"

From the weight room to the dorms, from the cafeteria to the locker room, wherever the Delaware State Hornets football team gathered in the winter following the 1981 season everyone was talking about Clarence "Sweet Feet" Weathers.

Weathers was an explosive receiver and running back who played for the Hornets in 1980. That year, he had 758 yards in kick returns on 37 attempts. Both of those marks remain the second best in Del State history. He had a 95-yard punt return for a touchdown against Salisbury State and a 100-yard kick return for a score against Central State. Nearly 40 years later, both are still school records.

His one season at Delaware State was so good that he was named first team all-MEAC while playing on a 2-and-9 team that was winless in conference play.

He was one of the players who left the school after Purzycki's arrival. After missing the entire 1981 season he had contacted Townsend and Purzycki asking to return.

"The kids were all buzzed up," Billings said. "They were excited about him coming back and that got us excited. We knew he could help us right away."

Weathers's brother Robert was a running back who had just concluded his college career at Arizona State and would be drafted by the New England Patriots in the second round of the 1982 NFL draft. Clarence Weathers was the younger and smaller of the two, but his explosive talent meant it was not unreasonable to think he'd eventually join his brother in the pros.

Weathers was scheduled to arrive in early January in time for the second semester. Bus schedules being what they sometimes are, the Greyhound carrying him from his home in Florida to Delaware arrived in Wilmington at 2:00 a.m. and Billings was tasked with picking him up.

"Don't ask me how I kept getting these wonderful assignments," he said. "I remember standing in the station and watching him step off the bus. He was wearing a velour sweatsuit and he had something on his head that I had never seen before."

Billings was looking at headphones attached to a Sony Walkman. He and Weathers swung by a McDonalds for some food and then drove back to Dover.

Billings had seen film on Weathers from 1980 and like any offensive coordinator (particularly one that runs the Wing-T) he could never have enough running backs. DSC had improved at running the football in 1981, and with most of the offensive line returning, the addition of a lightning bolt like Weathers meant the players weren't the only ones eagerly anticipating his arrival.

"Herky was so excited because we already had Johnny Rowe coming back and he had over 1,000 yards for us in 1981," Purzycki said. "Now we're adding one of the fastest kids from the state of Florida and he's going to have to figure a way to use him."

In the second week of January, the Hornets' off-season weight training program began. Once again, players were expected to be in the weight room at 6:00 a.m. three days a week. As the first week came to a close, Billings realized he hadn't seen Weathers at any of the sessions.

This isn't unusual. Some players need to be reminded that weight training attendance was not optional. Billings found Weathers and explained to him that he was expected to be there.

"OK," Weathers told him. "I'll be there, but I won't do squats."

Billings was irritated but Purzycki had put him in charge of running the weight training sessions, so for the time being, he decided Weathers was his problem.

"He would come to weightlifting and you could tell he had his own agenda," Billings said. Collick was at the early morning workouts and shared Billings frustration.

"We told every player, 'get in line like everybody else and get ready to get better,'" he said. "Sweet Feet just didn't want to do it."

"Then, about two weeks into the new semester, we found out he wasn't going to class," Billings said. "We were still building a new culture with our team and we had expectations. You WILL go to weight training. You WILL go to class. And we WILL be checking up on you."

Billings finally went to Purzycki to inform him of the situation. Purzycki met with his speedy-but-stubborn new player and, cognizant of his teams' need for talent, tried to reason with him about how things had to be.

"Clarence, you've got to do this," he began. "For starters, you have to go class. And when it comes to football, you can't decide what you go to and what you won't go to. We have to get stronger, Clarence. We're a bunch of weaklings and you need to come to weight training."

Weathers responded to his coach in the third person: "Clarence doesn't get up at six in the morning and Clarence doesn't lift weights."

"Well, if you don't start going to class, and you don't start showing up to weight training, you're not going to be able to be on the team," Purzycki responded. Weathers left the meeting unconvinced Purzycki meant business.

"He thought I was bluffing because he'd always done what he wanted to do at Del State. So, he continued to skip conditioning and he continued to miss class."

Coaches can and do make adjustments for star players and maybe at a different point in his career, Purzycki might have been willing to do so for Weathers. But they were still in the process of developing a culture of accountability at Delaware State and this was not the time the coach felt he could let things slide. Purzycki met with Townsend to inform him of what was happening and then kicked Weathers off the team.

Purzycki remembered something Philadelphia Eagles coach Dick Vermeil told him at his coaching clinic the previous summer: "Don't spend all your time on the squeaky wheel. You've got all these good kids over here and when you're spending time on the squeaky wheel you're neglecting good kids who want to be coached."

If the football team had been, in Billings' words, "buzzed up" about Sweet Feet's return, they were equally shocked when it was announced he'd been kicked off the team.

"That was the turning point in my mind," Billings said, "He got everyone's attention when he did that. You'd hear the players saying,

'If he's crazy enough to kick Weathers off the team, then he'll kick any of us off the team, too.'"

Purzycki thinks the turning point came later during the 1982 season but agrees that Weathers's departure was a big moment. His talent was undeniable. He'd end up playing nine years in the NFL as a receiver and return specialist after Robert Weathers convinced New England to take a chance on his brother.

"He would have helped us win," Billings stated flatly. "We'd have won a couple more games if we had kept him, but that would have been shortcutting our entire reason for being there. Kicking him off the team got everyone's attention."

Billings said the move paid dividends for a few years after it happened. After that, when a player wasn't going to weightlifting or class Billings would bring him in for a chat.

"Do you think you're as good as 'Sweet Feet?'" Billings would ask the player.

"No."

"And what did we do with him? We sent him home. If we sent him home, we're going to have no problem sending you home."

"Clarence Weathers is critical, whether he likes it or not, to our development," said Purzycki, "because when I kicked him off the team it planted a standard in the ground and got everyone's attention. They realized we were going to do it our way. From now on, the program was more important than the person."

That didn't mean there wasn't room for compromise with players who were willing to meet him halfway. Pat Spencer was a quarterback from Miami, Florida, who Purzycki had recruited off a tip from a former DSC player.

"An alum put us in touch with his high school coach who sent us some film. I took one look and I could tell Pat was a player," Purzycki said. "I called his coach to find out why a kid this good, from Florida of all places, hadn't gotten an offer yet."

His coach told Purzycki that Spencer had a few brushes with trouble in his high school career and that had scared others off. Purzycki decided to take a chance. "I knew once we got him on campus that he was a big-time Division I-type player."

Spencer emerged from a group of three players (Sam Warren and Bret Weber being the others) to become the primary quarterback for Purzycki's first team. Then, at the end of the season, he went home to Miami and didn't come back.

"It was very disappointing for all of us," Purzycki said. "He told us he was having financial problems and he had to go home to work."

Spencer returned to Miami where he got a job as a laborer in a nuclear power plant. Two months later, he called Purzycki and told him he realized that he had made a mistake. "This is not where I want to be," he said.

Purzycki told Spencer that he understood and that he'd like him back at Del State. But he also said Spencer would have to pay his own way for a semester, would have to work on getting his grades up, and if everything went well, he could rejoin the team after the 1982 season. "Show me you're serious," Purzycki said, "and we'll take you back."

That's just what happened. Spencer watched the 1982 Hornets from the stands before returning to become a key player in 1983.

By the time spring ball started in March of 1982 Purzycki and his staff were able to see and feel the signs of acceptance from a growing number of people within the DSC community. There were still doubters, but the list of people who recognized the good things that were happening within the program was rising.

Some of those people had been won over by a meeting with Purzycki shortly after he was hired. He asked Luna Mishoe if he could speak to the school's faculty senate.

Purzycki explained to the group that he knew the graduation rate among football players had been lousy. That led to a high dropout rate which made it hard for a coach to build the kind of consistency within a team necessary to be successful on the field. (At least 10 players from the 1980 team had flunked out of school.)

He explained his plan to institute a system that stressed academics and accountability, which was exactly what the faculty needed to hear.

"I thought that meeting helped me tremendously with being accepted by some of the professionals on campus," he said. "They saw that I had a good plan. This hadn't been a priority in the past. It was an obvious non-priority because the graduation rates were so bad. That meeting was an early positive thing."

Purzycki and his staff then put their plan into action and in their first season showed that the idea of stressing the student side of the student-athlete equation was going to be more than just lip service. That gained him more fans in the administration and with the faculty.

"There were plenty of people who stayed on the sidelines and waited to see what was going to happen," Purzycki said. "But there were people who jumped right in with us and made a huge difference."

Leo LeCompte ran the financial aid department, Jethro Williams was admissions director, Dr. Gladys Motley was vice president for student affairs, Maxine Lewis was DSC's sports information director, and Dr. James E. Lyons was vice president for academic affairs.

"The future of Delaware State College is right out on this football field," Lyons once said to Purzycki. "If we change the perception of the athletic program, we're going to change the public impact of this college. If we want to get alumni involved, we have to get the front porch in order because then they assume the rest of the house is in order."

Another influential voice and early supporter was Ulysses S. Washington who had coached the Hornets for two years in the 60s and was now the chairman of DSC's Department of Agriculture and Natural Resources. Also on board from the start was math professor Allen Hamilton who was also the chairman of the athletic council and had made the passionate speech in favor of Purzycki's hiring to the board of trustees.

"They were all people who saw what we were doing and wanted us to succeed," said Bill Collick. "We were allowed to stand on their shoulders."

The longer they were at Del State the better they were able to figure out ways to maximize what they had. "We haven't the money," Purzycki told his staff in an oft-repeated favorite quote from nuclear physicist Sir Ernest Rutherford, "so we've got to think."

Working with Townsend and LeCompte, they came up with a process to increase the number of scholarship players on the team. Players had to apply for a basic educational opportunity grant and a supplemental educational grant. LeCompte was in charge of the money and was allowed the discretion to use it as he wished.

"When we gave a kid a full scholarship, if the same kid qualified for money from one of the government grants, we'd use that money to cover part of the scholarship and use the money we saved to fund more," Purzycki said. "Collick had a great relationship with everyone in the financial aid office and that was a huge plus for us."

The effort to maximize every dollar they could get their hands on led to DSC being able to fund 75 scholarships, 15 more than Townsend had promised Purzycki when he was interviewed for the job.

"We started finding advantages where we could," Purzycki said. "We were innovative and creative in maximizing the resources we had. Nelson also helped me by finding summer school money for kids. That allowed us to have kids spread their workload out a bit. That's how other schools like JMU and Delaware were doing it."

It was a perfect example of why Townsend was so convinced Purzycki's extensive experience at Delaware would serve Del State well.

Expanding what was available was only part of the solution. The semester ended in May, but students didn't get their final grades until June, which meant coaches needed to be on top of players' grades and credits to know who to get enrolled in summer classes before the players even received their final spring semester grades.

"We got blindsided a little bit in the first year," said Collick. "We didn't get the grades until right before summer school started and we didn't have time to get guys into the classes they needed."

Enter offensive line coach Jeff Cannon with a solution.

Among his many interests outside football, Cannon was into computers and had vast knowledge of how they worked. The first guy Purzycki remembers who had his own computer, he approached the coach one day with what he thought was exciting news.

"The school uses Fortran computer programming language," he told Purzycki, who, like most of the world at the time had no idea what that meant. Cannon explained that since he knew how Fortran worked he was going to be able to monitor the players' classroom work, something that was not being done previously at Del State.

"He had figured a way into the school's system," Purzycki said. Not that Cannon could change grades, and Purzycki wouldn't have asked him to, anyway. The real benefits were indirect – they were able to get information about players' academic progress (or lack thereof).

"We were able to find out early if a kid was struggling academically and get him into summer school, so he could stay eligible," Purzycki said. "We didn't have academic counselors or resources to help players, so we had to figure out things like this on our own."

It was different from what he knew at Delaware. The Blue Hens had nicer facilities, academic support, more resources, and more money for any and all of those systems to help student-athletes.

"I had friends at the University of Delaware and I'd go visit and I'd see their dining hall, and how nice their facilities were, and we didn't have any of that," said Franz Kappel. "We were poor. But Coach Purzycki wouldn't allow us to use that as an excuse. He was constantly talking about how it was us against the world and we had to make what we had work. He made us believe in what we were doing. He put a lot of pride into us."

TWENTY

After 18 months at Del State, Purzycki was cautiously optimistic heading into the 1982 season. Enough starters returned on both sides of the ball that he felt his team was capable of continuing the upward trajectory and fulfilling his projection of doubling their win total to at least four.

Part of that optimism was rooted merely in the amount of time the players had invested in his program. In 1981, from day one, the players were expected to adjust not only to a new coaching staff but to a new offense that takes time, repetition, and discipline to learn.

"The Wing-T takes a lot of precision," said Billings. "That first year, we weren't very well polished, and it was apparent that it was going to take a while to get things rolling."

Some of the discussions he had with people regarding the progress of the offense left Billings shaking his head. Well-meaning friends would point out that Delaware State wasn't quite as good as Delaware running the Wing-T. Considering that the Blue Hens had been running the offense since Dave Nelson arrived from Michigan in 1951, the comparison rankled Billings.

"Delaware had been running it for 30 years, they had a freshman team, they recruited kids who had played in the Wing-T in high school. By the time Tubby Raymond got players, they knew what they were doing. I was trying to cook Thanksgiving dinner on Thanksgiving morning and he's had a year to prepare it."

But there was something else to the comments that bugged Billings even more. It was the attempted reinforcement of an age-old stereotype: White players are smart. Black players are athletic. It takes smarts to run the Wing-T and Billings was furious when people asked him how in the world he was getting black players to pick up on the offense.

"Of all the places I've been," he said, "the kids at Del State had the best football acumen. They picked stuff up right away. They had a knack for what we were doing. And they had a determination to get it right."

The Del State players heard the same kind of talk and it only served to motivate them more to learn the new offense.

"When you thought of the Wing-T back then you thought of white schools," said Terry Staples. "Black schools were going to win by using their speed. So now, we had to change the way we play and think, and that was a challenge that I was interested in taking. There was a strategy and a plan as opposed to going out there and just running."

"As we started to learn the Wing-T, we saw it worked," said Matt Horace. "It quickly became clear to be able to compete against schools we couldn't compete against before."

The Wing-T is a run-first offense, so it would be understandable if wide receiver Walt Samuels wasn't as enthusiastic about it. But as he saw the increasing success, he became a fan.

"I enjoyed the deceptiveness of it," he said. "People who we played against had never seen it and they had no idea what was coming at them."

The offense did at least two other things that helped the Hornets. Spending most of their practice running the ball naturally helped toughen their defense against the run. The coaches constantly preached to the defense that if they could figure out ways to stop the Wing-T in practice, it would be easier to stop the more basic running games favored by most schools.

It also served to bolster the credibility of the new staff.

"Coach Billings believed in the Wing-T more than anyone else and he made us all believe in it," said Franz Kappel. "He'd always tell us that it didn't matter if the other team knew what you're going to run, because as long as you run it hard enough and fast enough it's going to work."

"They were knowledgeable about the game and the strategy, and that got my attention," Staples said. "We found out that what they were telling us in practice wasn't just lip service. If we did what they told us to do, if we followed the rules of the offense: it actually worked, and it started making sense to everybody. That's what we'd been missing in the past. We had big guys, fast guys, and strong guys, but we weren't getting the detail stuff."

Before the 1982 season opener, the Delaware State football team got the kind of national attention heretofore unimaginable when *Sports Illustrated* sent reporter N. Brooks Clark to Dover for a story on the hiring of Purzycki and how things were going after the first season.

"We were looking for the man who best suited our needs," Dr. Luna Mishoe told the magazine. "That the young man happened to be white had *historical* significance. But from a practical standpoint it had no significance to us."

Purzycki told Clark that he was beginning to feel accepted on campus as "just a football coach" and related Townsend's comments to him from their first meeting about how he (Purzycki) was "going to have to see everybody's else's side of things."

The only player quoted in the story was Richard Williams who was among those players who wanted Billy Joe to get the job. "I was definitely concerned," he told Clark. "My main concern was his ability to coach the team. I'll say now that he's tough and he's fair."

The story closed with Townsend (as he had done all along) trying to move the discussion past the color of Purzycki's skin.

"One thing we were *not* guilty of was being color blind," Townsend said. "We were totally aware that Purzycki is white. But we were also aware that he'd be the best person for our program. The one thing I'd hope is that this will be the last interview I have to do on the subject of Joe Purzycki's being white. Because we have passed that stage. America may not have passed that stage. But we have."

Townsend would have been more accurate to say, "many of us have passed that stage." Because not everyone was done with the issue.

The offense had become crisper, and the defense had become tougher, but week one was going to be a big challenge: MEAC power South Carolina State, ranked seventh in the country in Division I-AA, would open the season in Dover. In his pregame talk, Purzycki reminded his players how far they had come and how different things were now for Delaware State.

"Everyone on this team was overlooked at some point and that's how most of you ended up here," he said. "But you've worked hard, and no one is overlooking you anymore. You've all earned the right to say to anyone, 'I AM SOMEBODY!'"

Purzycki then began quoting from a famous Martin Luther King speech that was actually written by Reverend William Holmes Borders Senior.

"I am somebody! I may be poor, but I am somebody! I may be young, but I am somebody! I may have made mistakes, but I am somebody!"

One thing that made Purzycki an effective speaker was his understanding of the importance of rhythm and cadence. The team fell in with him and the Hornets locker room was alive.

"We were grabbing each other," said halfback Ace Comer, "and screaming I AM SOMEBODY!'"

Sometimes pregame speeches have the desired effect. Sometimes they don't. On this day, South Carolina State rolled up twice as many first downs and almost twice as many yards as Del State. But the fired-up Hornets forced five fumbles, Comer caught his first-ever collegiate touchdown pass, and DSC pulled off a shocking 17-7 upset of the defending conference champions.

Purzycki called the game "probably the biggest win in Delaware State football history" and only half-jokingly said he planned to vote his team as the number one team in the country in the upcoming coaches' poll.

"We've been through hell," he told the *News Journal*. "We haven't seen too many good times, but maybe we will now."

In his game story, reporter Gene Bryson dredged up the Hornets' difficult past.

"Over the years, a huge black cloud has hung over Delaware State's football team. Drug scandals, ineligible players, and the 105-0 loss to Portland State scar the Hornets' past."

"This game puts an end to all that," said senior linebacker James Holt. "No matter what we do from now on, this game will be our biggest win."

The following week, the Hornets jumped to a 10-0 lead on Florida A&M, and for a moment they looked like they had built a complete team even far sooner than Purzycki had hoped. But that game turned into a 39-23 defeat, and their game one momentum evaporated. Still, to be 1-and-1 after opening the season against the two best teams in their league offered optimism heading into the third game at Division II West Chester State College.

Those feelings faded into the night when senior running back Johnny Rowe suffered a season-ending knee injury in the second quarter. Rowe was the second-leading rusher in DSC history and seemed poised to become the school's all-time leading ground gainer. But the injury ended his career and left the Hornets reeling since most of what they planned to do that season was keyed around Rowe running the football.

West Chester won the game 41-21 and the result so flattened Purzycki that he confronted for the first time a painful thought.

"We lose by 20 to a Division II team, my best player is out for the year, and my record after 14 games as a head coach is 3-and-11," he said. "For the first time, I had self-doubt about my ability to make it work at Delaware State."

Previously, any doubt Purzycki felt came from his concern that he wouldn't be able to overcome the barriers that came with being the first white head coach at an HBCU. This was different. Now, he was questioning his own ability.

He wasn't the only one.

Nelson and Diane Townsend made the short drive to West Chester to watch the Hornets play and were walking back to their car after the game when Townsend saw a group of angry Del State fans approaching.

"Uh, oh," he said to his wife. "You better get in the car."

Townsend wasn't afraid of a physical altercation. These were men he knew, they were friends of his, and they cared enough about the football team to have driven a couple hours to watch a road game. But they were mad at his head coach.

"Why did you hire him?" one guy shouted. "Why did you hire that white son of a bitch in the first place? Henderson could have lost this game just as easy. Why did we fire him?"

Townsend tried to be as patient as the situation allowed. He was still in Purzycki's corner, but these kinds of conversations and altercations were wearing on him.

"It was typical of what he went through," Diane Townsend said. "They did a whole lot of yelling and waving hands. They were upset that we lost the game. But it was never because we just didn't play well. It was always because of Purzycki."

Eventually, the fans got it out of their system and moved on, convinced more than ever that Townsend was wrong to have hired a white coach in the first place, and even worse, was a fool for hiring a white coach who couldn't coach a lick.

When Townsend and Purzycki met the day after the game there was a lot to discuss. Townsend told him about the post-game altercation with the fans. Purzycki felt sick to his stomach that his coaching led to Nelson and Diane having to go through something like that.

"I'm still under a lot of pressure about this, Joe. I can tell you're putting your heart and soul into this and I believe in you. But you get to go back to Shadow Court at the end of the day," Townsend said, referring to the street where Purzycki lived. "I'm dealing with the black community about this all the time."

Purzycki knew his boss was as devastated about the loss as he was. Purzycki's losses had become every bit as much Townsend's losses.

"He was saddled with me," Purzycki said. "I was his albatross. And just two weeks after a win that everyone thought had us rolling, we give up 500 yards to a D-II team and he and his wife are being yelled at in the parking lot after the game. I always appreciated all the crap Nelson was taking. The people who were upset about this didn't yell at me. Nelson was the lightning rod."

There was another more impactful problem at the moment that would ultimately affect Purzycki more than anything else he was dealing with.

Iron Mike Purzycki was dying.

TWENTY-ONE

Early in the week of that disastrous West Chester State game, Purzycki had received bad news from his brother. Their father had suffered congestive heart failure and was at the VA Hospital in Elsmere, about an hour north of Dover. Doctors told the family that his condition was critical, and recovery was a longshot.

"It was obvious from the start that he wasn't going to survive," Purzycki said. "The doctors were honest with us and we were in no way delusional. He wasn't pulling out of this. It was only a matter of time."

The coach spent the next several days shuttling back and forth between his team and the hospital. The overwhelming stress of his father's situation combined with the lousy performance in the West Chester State loss left Purzycki so frustrated that he unloaded on the officials after the game. At Townsend's suggestion, he sent them a letter of apology.

"I was so young, and I felt so much pressure. My team was struggling, my dad was dying ... it was so difficult," Purzycki said. "Nelson and I spoke almost every day for the next few weeks and his friendship was never more important."

The following week the Hornets had a game at Bethune-Cookman College in Daytona Beach. In the middle of that week, Mike Purzycki's heart failed again, and he was transferred to a VA hospital in Washington, D.C., two hours west of Dover. Purzycki continued to try to be two places at once: After practice, he would drive to the hospital, spend the night with his dad, and return to campus the next day.

Things stabilized a bit by the weekend and Purzycki consulted with Townsend before he decided to fly to Daytona Beach to coach his team in the game.

Del State scored the first three times they had the ball and jumped to a 21-0 lead early in the second quarter before Bethune-Cookman came roaring back with three scores of its own. Del State led 21-20 late in the third quarter and had to punt from its' own end zone. Bethune-Cookman's Wilford Morgan blocked the punt and for a moment it looked like the ball would skitter out the back of the end zone for a safety. But Morgan popped up, dove onto the ball, and was credited with a touchdown.

After their great start, nothing was going the Hornets' way. Kicker Everett Morgan drew DSC to within three with a field goal early in the fourth quarter but was just short on a 43-yard attempt in the final minute that would have tied the game. Bethune-Cookman escaped, 27-24.

Six days later, at 2:00 a.m. on a Friday morning, Purzycki got a call from his brother informing him that his dad was unlikely to make it through the night. Mindful of the stress he was under, Sharon Purzycki urged her husband to wait until morning to go to the hospital, but Purzycki immediately climbed into the car and made the trip. It wasn't until early Saturday that his father died. Purzycki was at his bedside when it happened. Mike Purzycki was 64 years old.

"It was devastating for me and the entire family," Purzycki said. "Like a lot of guys, I had idolized my father and he was a key figure in my life. Sixty-four is so young."

There is no good time to lose a loved one, but for Purzycki, the timing was especially rough. His job as a football coach meant he was evaluated on the basis of how his team performed on 11 autumn afternoons. Del State played Howard that day in Washington, D.C., and Purzycki wondered if he should coach in the game. Would his presence on the sidelines be an emotional lift to his team or would he be too distracted? Could he mentally, physically, and emotionally handle the pressure of coaching in a game the same day his father had died?

He discussed the pros and cons with his brother. "You hear guys say things like 'I played golf the morning after my dad died because that's what he would have wanted' and I found myself thinking that my father would want me to coach," Purzycki said. "I really was torn on what to do."

Finally, he called Townsend.

"I need your guidance," he said to his boss, his mentor, and his friend. "I don't know what to do. The athlete and the competitor in me wants to do it and knows my dad would understand. But I'm not sure I can handle it."

Townsend patiently listened to Purzycki. After all he'd seen, he had no doubt his coach could do his job. He also had no doubt about the decision Purzycki needed help making.

"You need to be with your mother, your brother, and the rest of your family," Townsend told him. "That's your proper place right now. We'll have other football games to coach and other Saturdays to celebrate. Be with your family now."

Purzycki was torn, but relieved. "I greatly appreciated what he did that day," he said. "I didn't want to miss anything with my family and I thought coaching might turn me into an emotional wreck. Nelson's wisdom took me off the hook and I never forgot that."

With Billings serving as head coach the Hornets again played well early, led most of the game, but lost 22-14. Purzycki and his family spent the day making arrangements for the funeral. He was at his brother's house that evening when he heard the final score.

He put football out of his mind and concentrated on his family before returning to work on Tuesday. At his desk, he began preparing notes and building a game plan for that week's opponent, North Carolina A&T, while pushing his grief away to be fully dealt with at a later time.

It's not as though the coach could push the "pause button" on the season.

As his focus returned to football, he wondered what had gone wrong with his team. The South Carolina State win and the giddy feelings afterward seemed like a dream. Four weeks after telling reporters he wanted to vote his team number one in the nation, four weeks after players vowed that Del State had turned a corner, they were 1-and-4 and vultures were circling overhead.

The Dover paper (the *State News*) had been fair with Purzycki during his first 18 months on the job, at one point coming to his defense after repeated attacks from the DSC student paper. But the new coach was now 3-13 and the paper ran an evaluation of where things stood.

The week after his father died, a story headlined "Purzycki Support Intact" contained the dreaded "vote of confidence" from his bosses.

"It made sense for them to ask that question at that time," he said. "But for me, with everything else I was dealing with, the timing couldn't have been worse."

The story began with the point that Luna Mishoe, Nelson Townsend, and Allen Hamilton (the head of the school's athletic council) were all still solidly in Purzycki's corner.

"Sure, you hear negative comments," said Townsend, "But I don't think there's a school in the country that's 1-and-4 where the fans all say, 'we understand.' People who come and pay to see the game pay for the right to be critical."

Mishoe, who still liked to remind Townsend that Purzycki was "*your* coach," was a bit more pointed in his evaluation.

"I can tell you this, I had hoped we'd be better in the win-loss column," the president said. "The coach set his goal before the year of having a winning season and I expect he's doing everything he can right now to achieve that goal."

Hamilton set a tone in the middle with his comments. He felt things were still on track and said he told players in his class that he still had faith in them, but he admitted that the results since the South Carolina State game had been disappointing.

"That story was fair," Purzycki said, "but it gave the detractors all the fodder they needed. You could feel them getting a little momentum. Their voices grew louder, and it was a real challenge."

Joe Lane remembered those on campus still not sold on Purzycki would gleefully taunt the players who were trying to turn things around. "They'd say, 'What's the white coach got you doing now? You guys are a high school team running a high school offense. You need to get rid of that white coach.'"

It was tough for Purzycki to ignore. But so was something else that was happening that week that served as a nice counterbalance to what he was going through. Each day brought a new round of flowers sent to his office and handwritten letters of condolence about his father.

The flowers and notes were from players. Purzycki constantly spoke about the team as a family. He often told his players stories about his own family, how they didn't have much money growing up, but they compensated for that with family dinners and huge get-togethers with his grandparents and his cousins. Family was at the center of everything that had happened in his life and he believed that re-creating that kind of atmosphere was *the* key component to success in a football team.

The wins weren't coming yet, but the players saw the value of supporting one another. That included supporting the coach. So, all week, flowers and cards kept arriving.

"I was so appreciative of that," Purzycki said.

The team then came together and responded with a 20-3 thumping of North Carolina A&T, ending the four-game losing streak. Senior cornerback Victor Heflin had 13 tackles and an interception to key what Purzycki called the "best game our defense has played since I've been here."

When Del State beat the Aggies the year before, the game ball went to Purzycki to celebrate his first win. This time, the players wanted to present the ball to someone they felt had an equal role in the ongoing effort to build the program into something about which they could all be proud.

They gave the game ball to Nelson Townsend.

"Townsend was a cool cat," Ace Comer said. "He reminded me of John Shaft. He was on the same page with Joe and he was on board with us. We knew he took a big chance on Joe and there was a lot of backlash."

Bill Collick was proud of the way his defense had played and thrilled that they chose to honor Townsend with the game ball.

"It took some courage for Nelson and Dr. Mishoe to do this," he said. "Nelson was able to get a lot of folks to open their eyes and see that a guy from the University of Delaware might be the perfect person to change the structure that had been in place at Del State for years. If I've got a neighbor, and his grass is better looking than mine, sooner or later I've got to find out why that's happening. I've got to ask him for help. That's what Mr. Townsend did when he hired Joe."

Had the players known what Mr. Townsend's next move was going to be, they might have given him more than the game ball. He was about to bestow upon Purzycki and the team a gift: a new player that he'd found through a series of events that can only be described as wildly fortuitous.

No one knew how good this guy was going to be. Shoot, no one even knew his name.

TWENTY-TWO

ownsend finished his lunch and began walking across campus on a hot afternoon in the summer of 1982. He needed to get back to his office for a meeting with a student who wanted to transfer to Delaware State and play football.

The player and his parents were visiting Dover to check out the campus and meet with Townsend to see what needed to be done. As he got close to his office, he squinted his eyes to make out three people coming from the opposite direction.

"John?" he asked. "Alice? Is that you?"

Indeed, it was. John Taylor and his wife Alice had been Townsend's classmates at Mary N. Smith High School on Virginia's Eastern Shore in the 1950s. They exchanged hugs and hellos and laughed the way you do when you unexpectedly bump into someone you haven't seen for a long time. Eventually, Townsend asked them what they were doing at Delaware State.

"This is my son, JT," Taylor said. "He's transferring here this fall and we're supposed to meet the athletic director and the football coach."

Townsend laughed at the series of coincidences unfolding in front of him. "I'm the athletic director," he said as he introduced himself to JT. "Let's head over to the office and I'll introduce you to Coach Purzycki."

His friend's son was small and as they all talked, Purzycki and Townsend exchanged glances of concern as to whether he was big enough to play college football. He had attended Johnson C. Smith University in Charlotte in 1981 but had been cut from the football team during the preseason, which was another red flag. Still, Purzycki was not in a position to turn away players: He needed all the help he could get.

They returned to Townsend's office and began the paperwork for JT to become a Hornet. When Nelson asked him why he had decided to transfer he explained that he had become homesick and he thought Del State would be a better fit.

John and Alice Taylor's son hadn't even planned to go to college. He got a job driving a truck for a liquor warehouse right out of high school. A few months in, he realized he was hanging around his client's establishments a little too frequently.

"I need to get out of here," he told his father, "or I'll end up no good." His year in Charlotte with the Golden Bulls had been a bust athletically but he got good grades and was able to transfer into Delaware State. The NCAA ruled him eligible to play in the sixth game of the 1982 season, but he could begin practice immediately.

He had been undersized his whole life and the equipment he was issued at Delaware State hung on his body like a trench coat on a toddler.

"My head was so small that I could almost spin my helmet completely around," he said. "My shoulder pads were way too big, and my pants sagged the way kids began wearing them in the 1990s."

The first time he walked onto the field for practice he heard other players laughing at him. They also laughed at Ace Comer who took one look at the new guy and piped up, "Who the hell is this reject?"

Soon enough they found out. Taylor was a quiet, likable guy who showed tremendous ability from the start. "You could tell when he walked on the field that he was something special," said Steven Holiday.

Assistant coach Walt Tullis decided that the J in JT stood for Jake. And Jake Taylor began working with the Hornets' scout team during practice.

One day, with Purzycki watching, the scout team ran a play that called for Taylor to run a slant from the left side. He ran the route, caught the pass, put a move on his defender, and sped upfield untouched.

"I come back to the huddle and they called the same play to the other side," he said. "I did the same thing. Caught the ball, put a move on a guy, and ran away from everybody."

"I remember his speed was just different," said safety James Niblack. "He'd get on you and he'd pass you. He was small and quiet off the field. But something happened when he put pads on.

152

He became a different animal and he got stronger and faster. It was like he flipped a switch. He was true to his craft and you could tell he was going places. I remember right away thinking he'd make it to the next level."

Linebacker Mike Colbert remembered something else about Taylor. After watching the new guy scamper past everyone on the defense, Colbert decided to put a stop to it. On the next play, Taylor caught a pass and Colbert zeroed in on him.

"He was a skinny, scrawny little guy," said Colbert, who would lead the MEAC in tackles that year. "But he was like running into a brick wall. He was the hardest player I ever tried to tackle. He was a beast out there, he was so strong. He was the best player I ever saw."

Taylor's debut as a Hornet came during homecoming against Virginia State. Del State trailed 14-7 in the fourth quarter when he got his chance.

"I came into the huddle," Taylor said, "and Rod Lester (the quarterback) looked at me and said, 'we're gonna run that slant pass you like.'"

Just like he had done with the scout team, Taylor caught the ball, made a move and rolled into the end zone for a touchdown to pull the Hornets to within one with about a minute to play. Suddenly, Purzycki was in position for back-to-back wins for the first time as a college coach and he wanted to go for it.

"I don't want to tie this game," he yelled at Billings. "I want to win it. Let's go for two!" Billings concurred that was the right move.

Purzycki shifted into Dutch Uncle mode: "Now Herky, I need a two-point play ... and it better be good."

"I've got a two-point play," Billings replied. "I don't know how good it is, but I've got one."

It was good enough to work this time ("Barely," Billings admitted) and lifted Delaware State to a second consecutive victory and third of the season.

The *News Journal* referred to the hero as "seldom-used freshman Jake Taylor," which was accurate although to be fair, he had only recently become eligible. The touchdown was his first on offense since his days as a pee-wee football star in the Pennsauken Youth Athletic Association (he had been a defensive back in high school).

He would catch three more passes that season and by the end of the year informed everyone that they had been calling him the wrong name all season. For some reason, Tullis got it in his head that Taylor was named Jake.

"Coach," he said one day in practice. "My name isn't Jake. It's John. I'm John Taylor."

As in John Taylor, who would go on to spend nine seasons with the San Francisco 49ers, earning two Pro Bowls and three Super Bowl rings, and catch the game-winning pass in Super Bowl XXIII in 1989.

THAT John Taylor. The one who would be selected to the NFL's all-decade team in the 1980s.

The players celebrated the win and those who had overheard Billings tell Purzycki he wasn't sure how good his two-point play was howled as they told their teammates about the sideline exchange.

Billings was popular with the players in part because he always tried to keep them entertained – providing a nice contrast to Purzycki's intensity.

"Every day in practice he'd do the same thing," Comer said. "We'd be in the middle of something and in his high-pitched voice he'd yell, 'Stop it! Stop it right there!' Then he'd look up at a group of ducks flying over the stadium. He'd pretend he had a shotgun with him. He'd hold his make-believe shotgun up and point it at the ducks and yell 'BOOM! BOOM!' He drove us all crazy."

Comer read that NFL legend Jim Brown would walk back to the huddle after plays. "It's the only time I can get my rest," was Brown's reason. If it worked for him, it should work for anyone, so Comer began walking back to the huddle. When Billings asked him why he wasn't hustling he told him that was when he got his rest.

"Ace," Billings said, "if you walk back to the huddle again you won't play for me again (here Billings paused and looked at an imaginary wristwatch which he may have kept next to his make-believe shotgun) until 1999!"

As Billings got to know Taylor, he found that his talented wide receiver smoked, so occasionally during practice or games, he'd offer to buy him a carton of Parliaments if he made a big play.

"He was that type of guy who made the game fun," Taylor said. "Some guys take it to the extreme and I understand the business aspect, but it's still a game. Billings knew that."

Billings had grown up in Middletown, Delaware, and all his life he went to school, hung out, and competed with black kids. It was all second nature to him, so he maintained that working at Del State was not a major adjustment for him.

Bill Collick was the same way. He had grown up in Lewes, Delaware, and from a young age, he saw sports as unifying black kids and white kids. There was a big playground in the middle of the town and kids converged there daily to play football, basketball, or baseball. After the games, they would find something to eat.

"We would go to each other's houses and the parents took good care of us no matter where we were," Collick said. "It opened my eyes at a young age. We found out that peanut butter and jelly sandwiches tasted the same no matter which neighborhood we were in and that really helped form my approach to life."

Billings didn't spend much time explaining his background to his players. Rather, he worked on instilling pride with an unwillingness to accept how things had been.

"When I got to Del State," Billings said, "I made a conscious effort to treat kids the right way. A lot of my players had come from impoverished conditions, they might not have had the best grades, and they were playing football at a place that had not had success and didn't have a lot to offer yet in the way of facilities.

"So, I *could* sympathize with them about all that. Or I could treat them like they should be treated. Coach them up with no excuses allowed. Because when you do that, you are saying to them, 'you are equal to any other person in the world.' If I made or allowed them to make excuses about anything I was just doing them a disservice."

Billings wouldn't allow players to call him "Sir," feeling that was too deferential. "Please me by doing the right thing," he would say to them, "not by calling me Sir." He allowed players to question his play calls and engaged in open discussions with them about why things were done a certain way.

"I always thought that if a player questioned a call it just means he wants to win as much as I do. We're all in this together and I wanted as much input as I could get. I didn't view it as criticism because they're the ones in the pit. They know more about what's going on out there than I do."

Things were looking up at Delaware State. But there was one more storm the team and Purzycki would have to weather, and it was the worst one yet.

TWENTY-THREE

After the back-to-back victories, Delaware State couldn't make it three in a row. The Hornets lost to Towson State 35-21.

It was another case of Delaware State playing well but failing to get the win. The 3-and-5 record was a slight improvement over the previous two years but "improving" only goes so far. At the end of the day, you either win or you lose. And losing, sustained over time, leads to frustration.

Despite the strides, the frustration was beginning to boil over.

Harold Young and Terry Staples were high school teammates from Saginaw, Michigan, who had arrived at Delaware State in 1980. They had been on the trip to Portland State and had experienced the program at rock bottom.

"We knew each other as kids," Staples said. "He was always the biggest guy around and he was always cracking jokes. He was a comedian. He'd talk tough sometimes, but he wasn't as tough as he appeared to be. His only drawback was that he'd get too emotional sometimes. He had a fire within and if someone made a mistake, he would be vocal about it."

Before the 1981 season, Jeff Cannon called Young the "fastest and quickest lineman I've ever coached" and praised his leadership skills. In the same *News Journal* story, Young said Purzycki's intensity and organization had convinced him he was playing for a coach who was going to start a dynasty at Delaware State.

But two years later they were still losing more often than they were winning and Young's voice was usually expressing displeasure.

"His raw emotion rubbed some people the wrong way," Staples said. "Sometimes, when you're vocal, that can be good. But Harold's fiery attitude affected people and may have caused some dissension within the team."

"Harold lived across from me and he always had an attitude about him," said Franz Kappel. "He never bought into what we were doing. It was like a running feud between him and the coaches. He was a good guy but that's just how he was. When we were watching game film the coaches would yell at us and he was the only one who would argue back."

"He had differences of opinion from time to time with the coaches, and that didn't work out well for him," Staples said.

"Harold Young was a hell of a good football player," Billings said. "But you can be a good player and if your attitude isn't right you can destroy everything."

Collick said flatly, "Harold had not bought into what we were about. I don't think it was about him not liking Joe. I think he was looking at it and thought, 'this is the same old bullshit. We're three-and-whatever, what's the big damn deal about this coach?'"

"Harold thought he could run the team but there's only one coach," said Joe Lane. "There were still people not buying in and Harold was one of them. He thought he was bigger than the program. He'd say crazy stuff."

Another player who didn't mind voicing his opinion was a sophomore safety from Florida named James Niblack, who said he allowed his feelings about the team to be influenced by outside forces.

"I was following and listening to some former players who had left the program. I had kept in contact with them," he said. "They wanted to stir the pot to see if the team would stay together as a solid unit. I was getting frustrated because we weren't winning, and I got it in my head that Purzycki wasn't the coach for us. I let others persuade me and I made a comment that I regret."

On the Monday after the Towson State loss, Niblack walked into the team's staff room where assistant coach Jeff Cannon was sitting. Cannon was working on notes for that day's practice and starting to develop the game plan for Central State, the Hornets' next opponent.

"Hey Coach," Niblack said, "The word around campus is you guys should be packing your bags because you're going to be fired. Are you getting a little nervous? I'd be nervous if I was losing my job."

Cannon was stunned.

"Get out of here," he snapped. "I don't need that kind of talk."

"I'd be jumpy, too, Coach," Niblack responded as he walked out.

Cannon relayed details of the exchange to Purzycki who was heading into a meeting with three other players who told him that they had grown tired of having Harold Young as a teammate. They said Young was a negative presence in the locker room. They had spoken to team captain Anthony Sharpe who suggested they see the head coach.

"That's the only time I remember teammates coming to me and complaining about a player," Sharpe said. "But he was being disruptive."

"They told me Young was telling people not to play for me anymore," Purzycki said. "They said he made disrespectful comments about the assistant coaches. It was all very ugly stuff."

Purzycki excused the players from his office and sat at his desk thinking about what they had said. Young was one of the best players on the team. He was a big, loud young man who as an upperclassman was in a position of leadership. Niblack was also a starter, a smart player, and a solid contributor.

After nearly two years, the Purzycki-led Hornets were 5-and-14. Cannon's exchange with Niblack, and the reports on Young made him realize that he still hadn't completely broken through.

The chirping had gotten louder in the wake of the *State News* story in which Mishoe had expressed disappointment in the team's record. "It didn't take much to get a hate fire started against us," Billings said.

At that day's staff meeting, Purzycki announced he was kicking Young and Niblack off the team. He then met with both guys.

Niblack was stunned but accepted the news.

"Coach Purzycki made comments earlier in the season that if we had a person who was negative or had a bad attitude, he would rather that person not be on the team," Niblack said. "I didn't take heed to it and I made an immature comment. It came back to haunt me."

Young denied saying the things he was accused of and asked Purzycki to reconsider but the decision had been made. "I'm sorry, Harold," Purzycki told his starting center. "We've decided to move on."

Significantly, Purzycki told both players they could keep their scholarships, but they were done as players at Delaware State.

(Young died in 2015 at the age of 53. "He was angry when he got kicked off the team," said Staples, "but it may have been the best thing for him in the long run. He learned a lot of lessons from it and eventually became more spiritual. He was a great father. He had five children. He was a teacher and a coach. He grew quite a bit from some of the turmoil and became a better person.")

Niblack waited a week to tell his mother the bad news. She was relieved when she heard he could stay in school. "Be grateful," she told him. "He's letting you stay and get your degree. So, do it. Become an asset to someone. I hope this teaches you a lesson about your mouth. I bet you keep your mouth closed next time."

Turns out, Niblack did just the opposite. He said that when he first left the team he became somewhat of a loner, but Frank Burton kept checking up on him and making sure he was OK. He and Burton talked extensively about the situation and what led to Niblack getting kicked off the team and Niblack started becoming an agent for positive reinforcement among his now former teammates.

"I told Frank, and I started telling other guys to not fall prey to the things that led to me being kicked off the team," Niblack said. "I listened to people who did not have my best interests at heart."

Niblack realized in hindsight what Purzycki and his staff were trying to do and what they were focused on. He told players that it was important to buy into the program and what they were trying to accomplish.

"But I didn't learn those things until after I was kicked off the team," he said. "I learned that you need to be careful what you say because it can be detrimental for you and your organization. Cancer like that can spread."

Niblack's goal became to create something positive out of the situation. He thought about playing basketball but instead took his mom's advice and focused on school. He got his degree in 1984 and later became a battalion chief in the Lakeland, Florida, fire department.

Purzycki left his office after meeting with Young and Niblack and went out to the practice field early and while waiting for the rest of the staff and team to get there he began to stew. He wondered if there were still guys in his own locker room trying to undermine him. By the time the team arrived, he was ready to get a few things off his mind.

"I was out here alone, waiting on you guys, and thinking about how much all of us have given to this program," he began. "I was thinking about how much everyone, Mr. Townsend, my staff, and many of you have given to the team. After all this work and sacrifice are we going to allow others to tear down what we're building?"

"I want you to think back two years ago when you lost 39-0. 52-0. 105-0. You were the laughingstock of the country. Two years ago, parents used to watch practice to make sure their kids weren't being physically harmed by the coaches. Remember that? Remember what it was like in 1980 when your coaches showed you no respect? Now think about what it's like today, and what we're trying to build here."

Purzycki had started calmly but his voice had been rising since he started talking and by now – "I just lost it" – he was screaming at his team.

"Did you think this would be easy? The strongest steel is forged in the hottest fire, but we have to go through that fire together. Someone on this team is going to question Bill Collick's integrity? Let me tell you about this guy. Bill Collick is one of the most respected men in this entire state and now he's got to put up with this fucking bullshit? He's one of the finest friends and mentors you will ever have in your life."

"I'm staying here, I'm going through the fire, and we're going to win. If you don't believe that, if you want to listen to small-minded people, then get the fuck out of my sight now. Because you don't have the strength or the sense to see what's right. I'm exhausted by everything we've put into this program. After taking on this reclamation project, this is what we get in return?"

Purzycki realized he had said enough. "It was a brutal few minutes. It was the most emotional speech I ever gave. All the frustration of the past two years was released."

After practice, Anthony Sharpe walked up to me and said, "Coach, I'm with you, and I'm offended you would ever worry about me."

Purzycki assured Sharpe that he believed him, and he knew his team captain wasn't the problem. He was spent and embarrassed and had reached the point where he felt he didn't have much to lose.

"I thought it was all unraveling," he said. "I thought it might be all over, but I was ready to draw my final line in the sand and fight for this program I believed in. I was ready to move forward, and I didn't care much for anyone who wasn't in the fight with me."

He remembered that on several occasions Townsend would tell him that he sometimes worried "a white coach might not be tough enough to put a shoe up a kid's ass when he needed it." Purzycki felt that at times he had been overly cautious about that, but on this day, his shoe had landed firmly between the cheeks of his team.

"The players really respected him after that," John Taylor said. "Both of those guys were decent players, but he was going to show you that he didn't care who you are or how good you are. If you can't respect the rules of this team and the way we're trying to do things, then we don't need you."

That Saturday, with less than seven minutes left in the game, Delaware State led Central State, 31-16. Purzycki figured his speech had had the desired effect. A Central State touchdown at the 6:33 mark cut into the lead, but a missed two-point conversion left the Hornets up nine. They appeared to have the game in the bag.

Del State took the ensuing kickoff and got to the Central State 41 when Purzycki elected to go for it on fourth down in an attempt to put the game away. They didn't make it. Still, it was a nine-point lead with two minutes remaining.

Central State scored on the very next play. Suddenly, the lead was two points with 1:45 remaining. On Central State's onside kick, two DSC players collided going for the ball, and the Marauders recovered. They scored three plays later.

The stunned Hornets inexplicably found themselves 37-31 losers.

Purzycki was rocked to his core. And what happened next could forever serve as a primary example of what it means to kick a man when he's down. As he walked across the field to shake hands with Central State coach Billy Joe (no less), Purzycki was shocked to see several *Delaware State employees* lift the victorious coach onto their shoulders and carry him off the field.

"That loss and the way the game finished gave fuel to the naysayers on campus who had been against us and in favor of hiring Billy Joe," Greg McLaurin said. "I remember Harry Moses (the school's director of intramural sports) was there. He had been an outspoken critic of ours and very vocal in his belief that the school should have hired Joe, and now he was helping carry him off OUR field."

"I remember seeing that," Mike Colbert said. "It was a strange sight to see people from Del State celebrating with the other team's coach."

"Dean Hicks ran one of our dormitories and had his arm around Billy and a guy who was one of our first-down marker guys was lifting him onto Dean's shoulders," Purzycki said. "I saw this happening and after the week we'd had, after blowing a huge lead and losing to the guy they could have hired instead of me, my insides were completely sucked out of me."

"This is a team I wanted to beat for a lot of reasons you guys aren't even aware of," the Central State coach told reporters after the game. He called it the biggest win of his career and acknowledged that the loss had to be heartbreaking for Purzycki. He stressed that his desire to beat Del State wasn't a personal grudge against their coach.

Meanwhile, the losing coach was slumped down on a cooler in the Hornets locker room. Every loss is bad, but this one left him gutted. He would second-guess himself about his decisions in this game forever.

Similar to his feeling after the West Chester State game, he found personal doubt welling up inside. For the first time, he was staring professional failure in the face. He thought about Tubby Raymond and his warnings about taking the job. He thought about his father, gone less than a month. He thought about Sharon, who had been a rock through it all but was now bound to hear people calling for her husband's job. The life of a coach's wife is tough. The life of a losing coach's wife is damn near impossible.

"Coach, Coach!"

Purzycki shook out of his stupor and looked up to see lineman Alfred Parham standing over him. It had been Parham who talked to him the day he was hired, following the first-meeting fiasco.

"You've got to get your head up, coach," Parham said. "The fellas in this locker room are with you coach. We're WITH you."

Purzycki felt tears welling up in his eyes. For the second time in two years, Parham had appeared at an absolute low point and had said exactly the right thing.

TWENTY-FOUR

While Alfred Parham's words after the game had given him a quick lift, nothing anyone said or did could fill the bottomless pit in Purzycki's stomach.

His defense had given up 21 points in less than six minutes. His decision to go for it on fourth down had backfired and was being second-guessed by anyone and everyone who saw it.

The Hornets' performance in the final minutes of the game left even his most ardent supporters shaking their heads. It was a collapse so epic it almost defied description: Up nine with three minutes to go, with the ball, only to fail on a fourth-down gamble, and go on to lose?

And then, when it ended, the nightmare continued: He had to watch Delaware State employees lift Billy Joe to their shoulders in a mockingly cruel gesture that he could not force out of his mind.

Asked why he chose to go for it rather than punt and pin Central State deep in their own territory, Purzycki said, "Honestly, the way they were moving the football, I don't think it would have mattered if we punted or not."

Asked about the keys to the game, he pointed to the onside kick Central State recovered in the final minutes of the game before their winning touchdown.

"All we had to do was field that and we could have run the clock out," he said.

Both comments irked Townsend, and when they held their weekly meeting, he calmly reminded his coach that he preached accountability to his team and had to show them the same in times of turmoil.

"I know you're upset," Townsend told him. "I know you're frustrated. But these comments sound to me like you're putting too much blame on the kids. To say that decision not to punt wouldn't have mattered makes it sound like you're not taking your share of responsibility for that call."

The coach nodded glumly and agreed with Townsend. No one had expected him to have everything turned around by now. But the lack of momentum, the inability to build on the mild successes they had achieved, the overall record of 5-and-15, and now the way they lost the game to Billy Joe's Central State team further backed Townsend into a corner.

He had done more than just weather the storm with his controversial choice of a head coach. He had absorbed the brunt of the criticism publicly and privately. In April of that year, when it became apparent that there was a potential boycott among HBCU schools to schedule games against Delaware State, he calmly replaced schools who balked at playing them with schools who would. He endured the constant jibes from Mishoe ("*your* coach lost another game"), and he spent evenings at home on the phone talking to friends (and others) who couldn't understand why he had hired Purzycki in the first place.

Still, he and Purzycki had been honest with one another since their very first phone call, and he saw no reason not to be honest now.

"Joe, with everything that's going on, I won't be able to defend you if we keep losing," he said. "A lot of people on campus are frustrated. A lot of our alums and fans are frustrated. The way people feel about things right now, I'm going to be hard-pressed to protect you if you're a three-win coach."

Purzycki was disappointed but understood and respected Townsend for his honesty. "He was direct with me, but in a very kind way. He knew it was eating me up inside."

Townsend had done everything he could possibly do to help Purzycki from the day he hired him. His support had been unwavering to this point, but it now came with a caveat, and no easy one at that: The Hornets had two games left on their schedule and Purzycki had to find a way to win at least one of them.

Northeastern had just three wins that season but had just walloped Central Connecticut 59-0. Liberty Baptist was on a five-game winning streak after an 0-and-4 start. Purzycki had promised four wins from his team in his second season, but after the surprising win over South Carolina State expectations had soared. Those expectations had long since evaporated. Now something good had to happen for him to keep his job.

"I understand," he told Townsend. "I know how brutally hard it's been on you to support me. And I appreciate all the people who have helped us. I don't want to let you down, I don't want to let those people down, and I don't want to let these kids down. I'll do my best."

He returned to his office and thought about all he and Townsend had gone through. He wanted to finish the job and to do so, all he had to do was do something Delaware State had not yet done. Northeastern and Liberty were non-conference Division I-AA opponents. Delaware State had never beaten a I-AA foe outside of the MEAC.

Dover radio talk show host Jack Costello used his show that day to weigh in on the Delaware State football program. Costello read a scathing indictment of Purzycki's tenure to date and concluded with a question for the DSC administration.

"Tell me, Delaware State," he said. "Why did you hire a white coach if he's just as bad as the black coach you had?"

That afternoon, Sharon Purzycki was at the supermarket with her two daughters. The Purzyckis had recently learned that a third child would be arriving in a few months. Her daughter Lisa was in the shopping cart while Laura stood next to them holding her mom's hand. As she waited for service at the market's meat counter, a former neighbor approached her with a sad look.

"Oh, Sharon," she said, "what are you going to do?"

"What are you talking about?"

"I just heard on the radio that Joe's being fired. What are you going to do, where are you going to go?"

Costello had finished his thoughts on Purzycki by concluding that Delaware State *should* fire him. The friend had mistakenly interpreted Costello's statement to mean that Delaware State had already fired him.

"What are you going to do?" she repeated.

Sharon didn't answer.

"That was a really bad moment," she said later. "I picked Lisa up and put her on my stomach, grabbed Laura by the hand, left my grocery cart sitting by the counter, and walked out to our car."

It wasn't until they spoke later that day that Sharon found out that her husband had not been fired ... yet. Meanwhile, at Townsend's house, Nelson relayed the events of the day to Diane.

"I'm hoping the guys will follow him," he said. "I'm hoping they love Joe enough to want to fight for him."

They did, but they would never know about the ultimatum. Purzycki told no one except his wife. For the team, and the staff, Northeastern was the next game on the schedule and that's what they were working on.

"I never knew any of that stuff had happened between Nelson and Joe," Billings said. "I had blinders on and I didn't feel the pressure. I kept thinking we just had to keep coaching our asses off. I didn't have to talk to Mr. Townsend, so I didn't have any idea of the added pressure we were facing. I was either too stupid or too focused to realize it."

Collick felt much the same. "I never thought about not being successful," he said. "I never thought we weren't going to get it done. Maybe I didn't know enough but I never thought that our jobs could be in jeopardy. I saw the improvement we were making, and I believed it was going to work. I may have been a little pie-in-the-sky."

Unlike Billings and Collick, Greg McLaurin sensed something was up during the staff meeting the night before the game.

"Northeastern had a lot of formations and a lot of shifting and since I was the defensive backs coach, I was in charge of our pass defense," McLaurin said. "They had this one shift where the tight end would trade sides of the field. I remember that night Joe was really hammering that home. Anytime that tight end moved we had to be sure we were sound to everything they did."

Finally, McLaurin interrupted Purzycki.

"We've GOT it, coach," he said. "We know everything they run out of that formation and we've got it."

Unbowed, Purzycki pressed on emphasizing that the Hornets could have no mistakes in the game. "Let's cover it all," he said, "again."

"The entire staff was perplexed because he was just on fire that night," McLaurin said. "He was beating me to death on that tight end trade to make sure we had it covered."

The next day, all the work paid off. Senior safety Tim Gray returned a blocked punt for a touchdown, and Dwayne Henry caught a 34-yard touchdown pass from Kevin Samuels as Del State grabbed a 12-7 halftime lead. It was 12 instead of 14 because kicker Everett Morgan missed both extra points. Before he lined up for a fourth-quarter field goal from 31 yards, special teams coach Walt Tullis had some words of wisdom for Morgan: "Everett, just kick the damn ball."

Morgan connected, and the Hornets led 15-7. The defense, which had burst like a weak dam against Central State, was stout at critical moments. Northeastern drove to the Del State seven but the Hornets stopped them on fourth down when Eric Harris, Craig Mayer, and Mike Colbert swarmed the ball carrier.

Colbert said that the staff's demeanor the week of the game was no different than at any other time during the season.

"No one could believe what happened at the end of the Central State game," Colbert said. "We had a regular week of practice, but the coaches kept emphasizing that we had to stay focused. We had blown a couple leads and they kept talking about how we (the defense) had to finish a game. That Northeastern win was a big leap for our confidence. It was a huge turning point for the defense."

"Some of our guys still had some residue on them from the past," Collick said. "But we were beginning to have great competition in our practices. We had young guys who were starting to push the veterans to be better and I knew it was only a matter of time before we put a solid performance together. That day, the defense played with real confidence."

In addition to his TD, Gray had an interception and six tackles.

Delaware State had the four wins Purzycki had promised and had a chance the next week to make it five in the season finale against Liberty Baptist. But even on a day when the Hornets rushed for an impressive 335 yards, DSC turned the ball over eight times and lost, 35-22.

The season was over, but all was not lost. "This team is stepping up the ladder," Purzycki said. "We've made progress. But now, we want to keep on climbing."

Most of that progress had been on offense. The Hornets were the second-best rushing team in the MEAC and the 20th best in the country in a season when top running back Johnny Rowe had been injured in the third game of the year. Fullback Doug Picott led the team with 664 yards rushing, but a bigger story was the emergence of a diamond in the rough named Gene Lake.

Lake had a breakout performance in the loss at Towson State when he had 130 yards on the ground, the first of 14 times in his Del State career he would eclipse the 100-yard mark. Lake had joined the Army out of high school and after that was playing in a recreational flag football league when assistant coach John Covaleski saw him and suggested Purzycki bring him in. Lake had two more years of eligibility and Purzycki and Billings thought he could become the bell cow they needed to run the Wing-T effectively.

Townsend and Purzycki never discussed the potentially difficult decision the AD would have had to make if the Hornets hadn't gotten to four wins. The South Carolina State win in week one had changed attitudes and expectations for the season, but in the end, Del State was right where Purzycki had told them they would be: They had four wins. The program was being run in a professional manner. Players were making steady academic progress and graduation rates were up.

What's more, they had the majority of their team back for a 1983 season, which Purzycki was certain would be their breakout year.

At the end of November, Townsend and Purzycki traveled together to the MEAC awards banquet. The guest speaker was Thomas Shropshire, the vice president of marketing for Miller Beer. Shropshire was one of the highest ranking and most successful African American business executives in the country. It was under his watch that Miller developed the concept for a new beer that would be called Miller Lite.

When Shropshire died in 2003 his wife told the Milwaukee *Journal Sentinel* her husband "believed in reaching back and helping others on the way. He didn't believe that once you arrived you forgot where you came from."

That was the theme of Shropshire's speech to the crowd gathered for the MEAC awards banquet in November of 1982.

"African Americans must bring the next generation along," Shropshire told the crowd. "We have an obligation to do it because white society won't do it for us."

"I was uncomfortable," Purzycki said, "But I kept looking at Nelson and it felt like every eye in the room was on him. Thomas Shropshire didn't know my story and I doubt he even knew I was there. His message was basically, 'We've gotta help each other.' There were plenty of people in that room who felt Nelson hadn't done that when he hired me, and it felt like they were all looking at him during the speech."

By now, Purzycki didn't need any more examples of the heat Townsend was taking on his behalf. But the incident served to remind him again that in the face of tremendous pressure Townsend remained calm and true to his vision.

There was another gathering after the season that was far more intimate and more important to Purzycki. In December, before his assistants went their separate ways for the holidays, they had a party at a small Dover bar.

"It was so poignant to me," Purzycki recalled. "Everyone brought something as a gift. I remember Jeff Cannon had these delicious loaves of bread he and his wife had baked for everyone on the staff. We sat and talked about the season, the crazy things that happened and lamented the games that got away."

As the evening unfolded, as music played on the jukebox and laughter and booze flowed easily through the group, Purzycki had a familiar feeling.

"I felt a tremendous closeness among all of us," he said. "We had become a family."

TWENTY-FIVE

Purzycki and Billings stood on the sideline looking at each other on a late summer night in Tallahassee, Florida.

The bulbs in the new scoreboard at renovated Bragg Stadium told the tale: Florida A&M 34, Delaware State 29. Just over two minutes remained, and the Hornets had the football on their own 15-yard line. Nearly 7,000 fans had come out hoping to see the famed Rattlers get a win, and it looked like they were going to head home happy.

Florida A&M had been an HBCU powerhouse for years, regularly producing NFL players (including Pro Football Hall of Famer "Bullet" Bob Hayes) and winning the first Division I-AA playoff tournament in 1978 under coach Rudy Hubbard.

"It felt like a different level of football," Purzycki said. "Everything on campus is painted orange and green. That's all you see everywhere you look. The fans were knowledgeable and into it. The band was as intimidating as the team. They'd stand behind you while you were warming up and they'd all hiss like rattlesnakes. The crowd would go crazy."

The crowd and band had enjoyed a shootout of a game that the home team was poised to win. During games FAMU fans often chant, "The Rattlers will strike, strike, and strike again!" and that's what happened, although every Rattlers strike had been countered with a Hornets sting as the teams traded the lead all night long.

Now, the Hornets had to go 85 yards or be pinned with a second loss at the start of a season that had opened with high expectations.

Their first game, a road loss at South Carolina State, left the staff and team furious. On that night, State College Stadium in Orangeburg was packed for the Bulldogs' season opener with fans who wanted revenge for Del State's 1982 win over SCSU. South Carolina State was the consensus favorite again in the MEAC (they would win the league title in 1983 for the ninth time in ten years) and the Bulldogs were picked in some corners as the No. 1 team in the country in Division I-AA.

The night got off to a strange start for Purzycki when, for the first time in his career, the officials refused to meet with him before the game.

"It's standard that the officials come to each team's locker room before the game to discuss rules that are being emphasized, what they expect of coaches and players, and to find out if you're planning on running any trick plays," Purzycki said. "On this night, the officials never came by to see us. When I approached the ref about 10 minutes before kickoff, he was dismissive."

The Hornets led 17-14 after three quarters but lost 24-17. They were whistled for six penalties in the fourth quarter, one an unsportsmanlike conduct call against Purzycki after he requested and was denied a conference for an explanation of a player ejection.

Purzycki was right, officials are supposed to meet with a coach when requested during the game – particularly after a player has been kicked out of the game. When his request was ignored, Purzycki earned the unsportsmanlike conduct penalty by waving his wallet at the officials while demanding to know how much they were being paid by South Carolina State.

Then, in the final minutes of the game, time was run off the clock – twice – after Delaware State called timeouts. "The whole fourth quarter was a fiasco," said Purzycki, who coached the second half in a shirt stained with soda that a fan had dumped on him when he walked out from under the stands at halftime. "We had control, we were moving the ball, but every time we did something good, there was a penalty."

Now, seven nights later, in another hostile stadium, the Hornets were staring at an 0-and-2 start if they didn't manage a late-game miracle. No one involved with DSC football was looking forward to explaining another close loss and another lousy start to another terrible season.

"Close anymore just isn't good enough," Purzycki had said to the *News Journal* after the opening defeat. "Playing a good game and losing is no damn fun anymore. Not in your third year."

Collick's defense had stopped the Rattlers' last drive and gave Del State's offense one more chance for the win. The defensive coordinator found himself feeling optimistic.

"There are plenty of times when you're coaching when you have that bad feeling late in the game that it isn't going to work out," he said. "That night, I had a good feeling the whole game. I thought by the end of the game they were on their heels and knew we were good enough to beat them. We had put expectations on our team and our kids now believed that we could do things like this."

Collick wasn't alone in his optimism. "Nobody would have bet on Delaware State to win that game," said tight end Terry Staples. "But by now, we had a bunch of guys who understood the system and we weren't guessing anymore. We were confident, and we knew what to do and that made a huge difference. It is amazing what confidence does. You stop worrying about how you're doing something, you just do it."

Quarterback Pat Spencer was having a great night for Del State. The Florida native had quit the team after the 1981 season but came back and spent 1982 doing the two things Purzycki had asked him to do: pay his own way for school and get his grades up.

Spencer's center was Nigel Dunn, another Florida native who knew how tough it was to play Florida A&M in Tallahassee and how big it would be for the Hornets to win there.

"Pat brought a different vision to our team at quarterback," Dunn said. "He and John Taylor brought a different mindset to our team and it started that night."

Spencer started the drive by hitting Taylor on consecutive plays to move the ball to the FAMU 41. But the Hornets stalled, and in the final minute they faced a fourth-and-six situation.

Spencer again found Taylor for an 11-yard gain to keep the drive and the Hornets' hopes alive.

Ace Comer made a one-handed grab of Spencer's next pass at the 13-yard line. Just 25 seconds remained.

Billings told Spencer to run "119 slant," which was a variation on the play Taylor had scored on twice back in his first Del State practice the previous season, and the play on which he scored the game-winning touchdown against Virginia State (when everyone still thought his name was Jake).

Spencer hit him mid-stride and, once again, Taylor turned upfield and dashed into the end zone lifting Del State to a dramatic 36-34 win.

"Pat was as good as we thought he would be, and he showed tremendous ability to get the ball to John," Purzycki said. "And that's the game where we all figured out John was going to be a superstar."

"Nothing about JT stood out until he was on the field," tight end Terry Staples said. "He had all the tools and from that night on, when we needed a big play, he was the guy. In clutch time, when you threw the ball to him, he was coming away with it."

FAMU had time for two plays after the kickoff, the final one being an incomplete pass into the end zone. When the clock wound to zero the Hornets had made a statement with a dramatic, come-from-behind win on the road against a tough opponent. It was the biggest win of Purzycki's career and ranks among the biggest in Delaware State football history.

"Our guys went crazy," Purzycki remembered. "Herky and Bill and I were jumping up and down, hugging each other, laughing and crying."

Before long, the trio toppled to the ground. They bounced up, looked at each other, and started jumping up and down again until they lost their collective balance and hit the deck again.

The players were the same way, running around the field in delirious joy. Before long, the impromptu party began to irritate people at the stadium.

"It was such a great game," said tackle Franz Kappel. "Florida A&M was the better team, but everyone on our team played above their head. We were so excited, but it was obvious they were not happy that we stayed on the field to celebrate."

The Florida A&M band traditionally performs a post-game show and they wanted to get started. But the entire Delaware State team was still dancing and laughing, and Mike Colbert remembers things starting to get testy.

"Here's how tough that band was," he said. "They were yelling at us and making threatening gestures. The band was getting ready to fight an entire football team."

As the celebration continued, someone at Florida A&M got the idea to douse the Hornets with the on-field sprinkler system: that would get the visitors to leave. Wrong. The exact opposite happened. Turning on the sprinklers reduced the Hornets to a group of five-year-old kids cooling off on a hot summer night. They ran through the spray laughing and enjoying every minute of what it felt like to win.

"We didn't mind the sprinklers," Staples said. "They had all that tradition. They had the best band in the country. They were a top-notch program and for a dusty little school like Delaware State to beat the Rattlers on their field was a big deal. We HAD to celebrate. We didn't have too many celebrations back then."

Eventually, the on-field party ended, and the soggy Hornets headed for their locker room. Purzycki and his staff followed and while the assistants got the group organized for the bus ride back to the motel, Purzycki met with the media.

"What does this win say about your team?" a reporter asked.

"When you are a 'have not' like we have been for such a long time you have to act like Avis and try harder all the time," Purzycki responded. "We are starting to grow up. We are not young anymore. We are maturing and that had a lot to do with our comeback."

"This was Pat Spencer's first big game in college. What did you think of his performance?"

"I thought enough of it that he'll be my nominee for the MEAC player of the week," Purzycki said. "We knew he was a big-time player when he was here in 1981 and we're glad he's back."

"Who is John Taylor?"

"He's a player who transferred to Del State last year," Purzycki laughed, "and after tonight, our number one priority is getting him more involved in the offense."

"Coach, it looks like you've turned things around at Delaware State. How have you had such success with black kids? How is that you seem to relate so well to them?"

Purzycki was taken aback by the question. He looked at his inquisitor and saw a young reporter who he surmised might work for the Florida A&M student newspaper. "I thought his question was inappropriate," he said. "But I also thought he was coming from a place of good intentions."

He thought about the question for a moment before answering.

"I'm a little bit offended that you'd ask me that," he began. "But here's what I'll tell you. At Delaware State, I've got kids with red hair and kids with freckles. I've got kids with afros. I've got kids from the inner city and I've got country kids. I've got kids who come from a poor background and other kids who have a little money. The success I've had is because I don't relate to any one of them in a different manner. You show me a person who does, show me a person who relates to people differently because of how they look or where they're from or what color their skin is, and I'll show you someone who is prejudiced."

He had handled the question perfectly, but afterward, it hit him that he had just experienced something he had heard his players talk about. When they would explain to him what they thought being black in America meant, they would tell him how they were viewed.

"Before I'm seen as a football player, or a good student, or someone involved in student government, or a musician, or a funny guy, or a handsome guy … before any of that, many white people see me first as a black man. And that's how they'll always see me."

Purzycki never grasped the full meaning of that statement until that night in Tallahassee. But at that moment, it hit him that he was in a similar, if not reversed situation. Before he was seen as a football coach, or an educator, or a motivator, before he was seen as any of that, by some black people he would always be seen first as a white man.

"I was still the white coach at the black school," he thought. "And for some people, that's how they'll always see me."

His press obligations concluded, Purzycki boarded the team bus for the ride back to the motel. It was after 11 p.m. when they arrived. "It was a classic, old-style Florida motel, built so that every room faced the pool," he said. "The players got off the bus and cut through the pool area to get back to their rooms."

Yeah, that's right. They were all going to go past the pool to their rooms.

"We weren't in there ten seconds before somebody pushed somebody into the pool," Billings said. "We were all still so elated. We knew we were good and to win at FAMU validated that. Before long, every player was in the pool. Some of them hadn't bothered showering after the game and still had their uniforms on. It was absolute chaos."

As the players laughed and splashed at their impromptu pool party, rooms lit up and curtains were yanked back by motel patrons who had already called it a night.

"All of us were hootin' and hollerin' and raising hell," Billings said. "I remember the manager of the place came out and he was furious."

"Get these guys out of the pool and under control," he yelled at no one in particular. "I've got people who are so mad they're going to check out. Quiet down! Out of the pool!"

Purzycki normally would have been right behind the manager screaming at his players to quiet down. But for now, he let them enjoy their win. Many times over the past few years these players felt the sting of defeat. They had been blown out. They had lost close games. They were all well-versed in how that felt.

But tonight … tonight it was Delaware State's world, and as far as Purzycki was concerned everyone else could just watch the party.

"It's one thing to accomplish something," said Staples, one of those who survived the 1980 Portland trip. "It's another thing to come from nothing. That's what it felt like we had done."

TWENTY-SIX

ownsend was sitting at his desk the Monday morning after Del State's homecoming win over NC A&T and was startled to hear Purzycki shouting his name as he ran down the stairs and into the hall that separated their two offices.

"Nelson!" Purzycki yelled. "You have GOT to see this!"

The coach was breathless by the time he ran into Townsend's office and handed him the just-released Division I-AA Top 20 rankings for the week of October 17, 1983.

Purzycki had frantically scribbled the teams and their respective rankings onto a piece of paper as they were relayed to him over the phone by Jack Ireland, who had just seen them on the *News Journal*'s Associated Press wire.

There, at number fifteen, sat the Delaware State Hornets. For the first time in school history, the football team was ranked in a national poll. Mr. Townsend and the Polish Prince wore huge grins as they looked at each other.

"As thrilled as I was," Purzycki said, "as proud as I was, Nelson mirrored my enthusiasm. Our success meant as much to him as it did to me."

Among the teams ahead of them was the only team to beat them thus far in 1983, South Carolina State. Purzycki was still a little salty about that defeat and how things went down in the final minutes of the game. But that was easier to set aside with this piece of great news.

It was a little over a month since the comeback victory over Florida A&M. That game and its emotional aftermath had been the start of what was now a five-game winning streak for DSC. The following week, they enjoyed their first ever-rout under Purzycki, a 56-6 pasting of the University of District of Columbia. Then, after a 23-16 triumph over Bethune-Cookman (preserved when cornerback Billy Alston knocked down a pass in the end zone on the game's final play), the coach first lobbied for his club in the polls.

"I think we're deserving of national recognition," he told the *News Journal*, "we're deserving of being ranked."

The following week, again at home, the Hornets played James Madison University for the first time. The Dukes arrived in Dover led by two future NFL stars. Defensive lineman Charles Haley was destined for the Pro Football Hall of Fame, but it was wide receiver and return specialist Gary Clark who garnered most of the pre-game buzz.

Three weeks earlier Clark had returned punts 87 and 89 yards for highlight-show touchdowns against Division I foe Virginia. Virginia ended up winning the game 21-14, but Clark's electric performance was widely noticed. The Dukes were talented and deep and presented DSC with another major challenge.

"They were for real," Purzycki said. "We had not beaten a team of this caliber."

Clark was spectacular, with seven catches for 185 yards and a touchdown against the Hornets. But he wasn't the best player on the field. That was Taylor, who scored four touchdowns: three on catches totaling 150 yards, and another when he ripped a page from Clark's playbook with a 68-yard punt return. In the end, it was a 38-28 Delaware State triumph. Between them, Taylor and Clark would go on to win five Super Bowls and play in six Pro Bowl games. It's doubtful Alumni Stadium ever saw two more dazzling performers on the same day.

Haley made his presence known, or at least felt, too. Ace Comer came to the sidelines after one series of downs rubbing his jaw.

"Haley punched me in the jaw," Comer said to Purzycki.

One of the regular themes of Purzycki's talks to the team was about how as an undersized kid he had been picked on by bullies. The bullies had finally relented when Purzycki fought back. He'd use that theme for the entire team. "You guys have been the small kid in the neighborhood for too long," he'd told them countless times. "We're fighting back now, and the bullying is over."

So, Comer's complaint about Haley was met with a quick rejoinder from his coach.

"Tell one of the linemen," he barked at Comer. "Tell them to hit him back."

Led by junior Franz Kappel and senior Nigel Dunn, the Hornets offensive line had become the kind of formidable foe that was literally and figuratively punching people in the mouth each week. Kappel had become an anchor at tackle and was on his way to becoming the first white player ever to be named to a Historically Black Colleges and Universities All-American team. Dunn had become a team leader at center.

("Franz was a quiet leader," Dunn said. "I was more like an annoying little brother.")

Billings set the record straight on that score: "Nigel's leadership in that third season was what helped us turn the corner. He had the respect of the players and he was tough and smart. He became our captain and he'd constantly step in and tell a guy, 'This isn't how we do things here.' He was a guy who solidified things for us."

One of the ways Dunn did that was by forming a group he called The Football Club. The Football Club came into existence after the 1982 season because Dunn wanted the team to get together for non-football activities. They put on a Chippendale's style dance show for fellow students. They formed teams together for the intramural basketball league on campus. They attended parties and went to clubs as a group.

"A lot of it was just silly stuff," he said. "But it drew us all closer together and helped us become a team."

Dunn would go on to a successful coaching career in Florida high school football, and – much like Purzycki taking mental notes as a player 15 years earlier on how Tubby Raymond was doing things at Delaware – Dunn watched Purzycki and picked up ideas he would use with the teams he eventually coached.

"I was destined to be a coach and I already had a coaching mindset," Dunn said. "I learned a lot from him about how to be organized and how to motivate. He and the staff were always putting up signs in the locker room with little tips about players on the team we were getting ready to face, or motivational sayings."

Players might arrive at practice to find a picture of the guy they were facing that week in their locker. The accompanying note would list the player's strengths and weaknesses and would mention anything he had said in the media that might be perceived as a slight or used as motivation.

"The coaches always gave us the sense that we had the opportunity to win and that helped the attitude of the team," Dunn said. "My first year (1980) players would sit around talking about how bad we were going to lose that week. I had played on a successful team in high school and that attitude was something I wasn't used to. I really appreciated that Purzycki always talked about how we were going to win."

Interestingly, he disagreed with the decision Purzycki made the previous season to kick Harold Young off the team even though that decision made Dunn a starter.

"Harold said things that could rub people the wrong way at times," Dunn said. "We would work out together and he'd always tell me, 'You're weak! You ain't ever gonna play, Dog.' I was his friend and that's how he talked to me. It's just how he was. If I was the coach, I wouldn't have liked what he said but I thought it was just a case of a young man saying something foolish and I wouldn't have kicked him off the team."

Kappel's DSC career got off to a shaky start after that blown assignment near the goal line late in his first game his freshman year against Virginia State. The following week at South Carolina State, he was so overwhelmed that he approached Billings and asked to be taken out of the game.

"Oh, you wanna come out, do you?" Billings said. "Well, let me tell you what we're going to do. You're going to stay in there and you're going to keep working and you're going to learn from these mistakes. Like it or not, you're one of the best eleven we've got."

Billings saw Kappel's promise in 1981, and by 1983 it was Kappel who routinely made other guys look foolish. He, Dunn, and the rest of their unit all benefitted greatly from line coach Jeff Cannon, who bore an uncanny resemblance to comic-strip sportscaster Tank McNamara.

"He was a big friendly guy," Kappel said. "He was always confident in himself and in us. He was a great teacher and he was really good at getting his points across and helping you overcome weaknesses. He believed in what he was doing, and when a coach believes, eventually the players believe."

"He treated the backup guys like they were starters," Dunn said. "When he talked to you, you could tell he wasn't bullshitting you. I admired him more than anyone else on the staff and I imitated a lot of what he did in terms of preparation when I became a coach."

Cannon usually was mild-mannered so when he did get upset players knew it wasn't for show. Kappel says the offensive line gave Cannon feedback once on his approach to being angry.

"During a practice in 1983, when we were getting better and there was a little more pressure on all of us, he snapped and starting cussing at us. But he didn't really know how to cuss. He was too nice a guy. So, everyone just started laughing at him."

"Don't do that anymore, coach," his players laughed at him. "You're not good at it."

With the players now fully bought in, with the Hornets' running game now statistically among the nation's best, and with Spencer and Taylor emerging as a quick-strike duo, Delaware State had emerged. The win over JMU was followed by a 26-7 rout of NC A&T that left the Hornets at 5-and-1, which resulted in Purzycki standing in Townsend's office while they relished the team's Top 20 ranking.

"We were now exceeding our own expectations and it felt great," Purzycki said. "I remember thinking that this must be what it feels like to have a hit record."

Imbued with the personality of a head coach, Purzycki's enjoyment and pride at the moment was tempered by the reality of the non-stop grind of the football calendar. The Hornets faced a powerful Liberty team in six days and the coach told Townsend the Flames' motivation would be increased since they now had a chance to beat a ranked team.

Townsend agreed but reminded his head coach to appreciate what had been accomplished. "This means a great deal to me, and it means a great deal to the school. Enjoy it, Joe. This is a big day for you, and for Delaware State."

When he met with reporters about the news a few hours later, Purzycki kept his eyes focused ahead.

"For all the things we've had to do to build the program, it's very important to get this kind of recognition," he said. "It's very prestigious and a shot in the arm for all of us. Now, we have to maintain our consistency to stay in the rankings."

Purzycki spent the week reminding his players that beating Liberty would ensure the Hornets a winning season. He told them to be proud of the national ranking but reminded them that it meant they were a bigger target. He worried and fretted and did the things a coach does before he walked into Lynchburg City Stadium on a rainy Saturday afternoon ... and promptly watched his team turn in one of the greatest performances in DSC history.

The Hornets set Del State records that day for rushing yards in a game (463), first downs (30), points in a quarter (28), points in a half (42), and total yards (624) in a 48-24 rout of Liberty.

Spencer opened the onslaught on the game's third play with a 56-yard scoring strike to Taylor (still referred to as "Jake" in newspaper accounts of the game). Fullback Gene Lake rushed for 178 yards and two touchdowns.

Comer had 93 yards and a touchdown. The kid from West Philly who had walked into a door on his first day at the school in 1981, drove the other running backs crazy because when he brought in plays from the sidelines he'd often switch himself into whichever halfback slot was going to carry the ball.

"I would send Comer into the game," Billings said, "and I'd tell him we want to run sweep right. Dwayne Henry would be the left halfback, so he was supposed to get the ball. But Comer knew both positions, so he'd get to the huddle and tell Henry, 'Coach told me to tell you that you need to switch over to right halfback and we're running sweep right.' I'd look up and Comer would be running the ball and I'd think, 'How did that happen?'"

On this day, there was plenty of work for everyone. Henry matched Comer with 93 yards. Steven Holiday (another regular victim in Comer's "coach said for you to switch sides" game) had 23 more and a touchdown.

The defense scored when linebacker Andre Williams returned an interception for a score (one of five picks by the Hornets). Williams also recovered a fumble later in the game.

"We were starting to see the fruits of our labor," Collick said. "We had been in games where we had trouble scoring, or even getting a first down. We had been in games where the defense couldn't stop the other team. That day, everything came together."

"By now, we were holding ourselves accountable," Holiday said. "We started getting in each other's faces when mistakes were made. No one took it personally, it was just maturity as a team. We'd run plays so often in practice that we had a complete understanding of how the offense was supposed to work."

As the Hornets rolled north toward Dover aboard the Gray Ghost, they laughed and joked and soaked in the feeling of being winners. When they next gathered for practice on Monday afternoon, they were ranked as the 12th best team in Division I-AA.

Better than that, they were now a group about which the entire school was excited.

"Everything had changed by that point," Purzycki said. "We were all part of the Delaware State community. We were accepted, and you could feel that everyone was proud of us. It was an amazing change."

TWENTY-SEVEN

"**S**ame old Del State! Same old Del State!"

If there was a team in the MEAC that would remain skeptical of Delaware State's newfound success in football it would be Howard University. The Bison were the Hornets oldest rival (dating to 1941) and they had owned DSC for more than a decade, with 11 wins in the 12 games from 1970 to 1982.

So, when the Bison players began chanting "Same old Del State" before the game, it certainly didn't come as a shock to the Hornets. It was irritating, nevertheless, at least partially because the Bison had recent evidence that their chant might be true.

The Hornets had hit upon tough times after their big win at Liberty. They lost by a touchdown to Towson State the next week thanks to eight turnovers. "We just gave that game away," Purzycki said. He was surprised that the Hornets maintained a national ranking (slipping to 17th) after the loss had dropped them to a 6-and-2 record.

The following week, they again gave the football away eight times and lost to Billy Joe and Central State, 49-26. The Marauders were 9-and-0 after the win and were destined to reach the 1983 NCAA Division II championship game (eventually losing to North Dakota State).

Del State snapped its two-game losing streak, sort of, the next week in Boston with a 21-21 tie against Northeastern, salvaged when Spencer led them 80 yards into a 25 mile-an-hour wind in the game's final minutes. "They say it's like kissing your sister," Billings said, "but that's better than kissing your dog."

So, their 6-and-1 start had turned into a 6-3-1 record with the Howard game left to play, leaving Del State's players in no mood to hear anything about the "same old Del State."

"You heard them," Purzycki said in his final address to the team before kickoff. "They think you're the same team they've always beaten. They think you're the same team they've pushed around for years. They don't know what everyone in this room knows. They don't know how much work you've put in and how much you've improved. They think you're the same old Del State."

Purzycki had talked to his team all week about ending the season on a high note. He compared their last game to the punctuation mark at the end of a sentence. "Do you want to end this season with a period, a question mark, or an exclamation point?"

Maybe he should have said exclamation points.

With the game tied at seven in the second quarter, the Hornets scored four touchdowns in the final six minutes of the first half as the team's frustration from the past three games popped like a champagne cork. They led 34-7 at halftime, 55-7 after three quarters, and won the game 62-20. The 62 points were the most scored by a Delaware State football team since 1950.

What a way to end a season!

Tight end Terry Staples was playing in his final game as a Hornet.

"You could see how we had progressed," he said. "Howard just couldn't stop us at that point. We had such an arsenal, and once we got up, we wanted to keep it going. They had put a little fire up under us with that 'Same old Del State.' thing. We weren't the same team everyone used to joke about, and we wanted to win by as much as possible."

John Taylor had one of his pick-your-poison kind of days. He scored on a 73-yard punt return, he caught a touchdown pass from Spencer, he scored on an end around, and he even fell on a fumble in the end zone for another TD. His 13 touchdowns in 1983 set a Delaware State record.

The Hornets defense had five interceptions, including one by linebacker Mike Colbert. "By the Howard game we had really jelled as a team," Colbert said. "We had a good nucleus of camaraderie and spirit. Coach Purzycki had instilled in us the ability to believe that we were just as good as any school, and by the end of 1983, we all believed that."

Fullback Gene Lake capped his year with 96 yards and a pair of nine-yard touchdowns. He became the second player in school history (and in Purzycki's tenure) to eclipse 1,000 yards in a season, joining Johnny Rowe who had done it in 1981.

"I guess they found out we're not the same old Del State," Lake told the *News Journal*. "I went out and got 1,000 yards and broke Johnny Rowe's record. I feel really good about it."

Senior Nigel Dunn started and played most of the game at center despite a sprained ankle sustained the week before at Northeastern. Late in the game, Billings approached him and thanked him for staying with the team.

"If you hadn't stepped up and been a great leader," Billings said to the team captain, "we would never have enjoyed this much success."

"It was a good way to go out," Dunn told Gene Bryson of the News Journal. "I thought about quitting (in 1981) but then Coach Purzycki came and he brought a lot of good things, so I thought I'd stick it out. I just wish I was coming back because I'll miss out on all the fun next year."

Purzycki enjoyed the day, too. "Same old Del State, huh?" he crowed on the sidelines late in the game. "Same old Del State!"

They had celebrated after season-ending losses in 1981 and 1982 because they had so many players coming back and felt they were only going to get better. Now, with 19 of their 22 starters back in 1984 and a final victory to celebrate, there were no more qualifications on the success they were enjoying. The giddiness level in the locker room was so high that Purzycki and his staff were dragged one by one into the showers by players who gave each coach a fully clothed celebratory soaking.

"There was a euphoria about that game that I'll never forget," Purzycki said. "The public perception was changed, and people were proud of Delaware State. Everyone was patting me on the back and shaking hands. All the barriers were broken down. What we had to go through in '81 and '82 was so tough and when we came out of it we were ready to roll. We won all these games in 1983 and after that, I never had to address race again. We had overcome our differences and all the bad stuff was behind us."

Almost all the bad stuff. There was one more bad thing that had happened in 1983 that made some of the other stuff look pretty menial by comparison.

The Central State game on November 5th had been an exercise in frustration for the team. Three fumbles, five interceptions, and a slow start all added up to a 49-26 defeat.

It had been a frustrating day and it would have a long ending as DSC faced a 10-hour 600-mile bus ride home to Dover. By the time the players finished their post-game dinner it was almost 7 p.m. If all went well, they'd get home around sunrise.

They were on Interstate 70 in Maryland between Hagerstown and Frederick at about 3:30 am when everyone on board was suddenly wide awake.

"I was sitting next to Bill Collick and I was trying to sleep," Billings said. "I had my head on the railing between me and the bus driver. I remember hearing the brakes screeching and then BOOM. And then another BOOM!"

Del State's driver was a guy everyone called Pork Chop. "He had huge pork chop style sideburns," Billings explained. "Every kid on our team had a boom box on trips to listen to music and Pork Chop used to yell at them, 'Keep that bongo music down, it's getting on my nerves.' The kids loved him, and he was a good bus driver."

Pork Chop was summoning up all his skill now, steering the Gray Ghost back and forth into the skid to keep the bus from spinning around or flipping over. Meanwhile, players startled awake with no idea of what was happening were screaming in terror.

"I thought maybe someone had taken a shot at us, or thrown a rock on us," Billings said. There were several different trucker strikes throughout the US in 1983 and sometimes buses and trucks on the road during those strikes were attacked. "Then, I thought maybe we had run up over a car."

Pork Chop finally brought the bus to a stop and grabbed his CB radio.

"Breaker, breaker!" he shouted into the mike. "This is Pork Chop. I'm in a stagecoach and I just hit two horses!"

Billings was unfamiliar with CB jargon and had no idea what Pork Chop was saying. All he heard was "stagecoach" and "horses" and he thought his driver might be having hallucinations about the old west.

188

"Dammit, Pork Chop!" Billings yelled. "Knock it off with that CB crap. Tell them we've been in an accident."

Turns out, that's exactly what Pork Chop had done. A bus, in CB slang, was a stagecoach. And Pork Chop was the only one on board who knew that his stagecoach had, in fact, just hit two horses.

With the notable exception of the horses (rest in peace) no one was hurt. "I take my hat off to Pork Chop for that," Steven Holiday said. But it took several minutes for everyone to calm down. The crash had completely wiped out the bus's electrical system so there was no light anywhere. The air in the bus stank of burned tires, burned brake pads, and horse shit.

Making matters worse, no one could get off the bus because the collision had crushed the front door and windshield. On many Del State trips aboard the Gray Ghost, the steps in the door well served as a sleeping area for a coach. Fortunately, on this one, no one was sitting there when the collision occurred.

A van with a few support staff members had been following the bus. Purzycki gave them money through an open window and instructed them to go get food for everyone. (Somewhere in Western Maryland lives a person who remembers the night when a guy wearing a Del State hat walked into the all-night McDonalds at 4 a.m. and asked for seventy orders of pancakes.)

Other drivers heard Pork Chop's call for help and radioed the police. When the Maryland state trooper arrived, he was able to pry the door open from outside to the point that he could get on. Once he ascertained everyone was OK, he pulled out a stack of papers and announced that since there had been an accident, everyone involved had to fill out a form.

He added an instruction that spun heads the length of the bus: "You've all got to fill this out completely … I need your name, where you're from, and whether you're white, or colored."

Despite the fact that the word appears in the very title of the NAACP, sociologists, historians, and linguists agree that most people stopped using it by 1970. The cop's use of the word with an accompanying arrogance caused a buzz to ripple through the players. Freshman linebacker Obbie Maull jumped off his seat and stepped in the aisle. "There ain't no colored on this bus," Maull angrily announced.

"I wanted to punch the cop in the mouth," Billings said. "WE had been in an accident and his tone made it seem like we had done something wrong."

Beyond the comment, the air was thick with the question: "How in the world would skin color matter?"

John Taylor reasoned, "The quicker we get the forms filled out, the quicker we can get going," and players at the front of the bus grabbed a form and passed the remaining ones back. Then, as order was almost restored the unmistakable voice of comedian Richard Pryor came booming out of one of the players' stereos.

"PUT YOUR HANDS UP, TAKE YOUR PANTS DOWN AND SPREAD YOUR CHEEKS!"

It was one of the lines from a classic Pryor bit about how African Americans felt police routinely dealt with them. The bit is from a show Pryor did in 1974. This was 1983. A player had cued the tape and let it rip. There was a moment of silence before every player and coach on the bus exploded in laughter. As they quieted down, here came Pryor's voice again, in an exaggerated, pronounce-every-syllable-clearly voice meant to convey the fear blacks felt when stopped by police.

"I AM REACHING INTO MY POCKET TO GET MY LICENSE."

Again, big laughter filled the bus.

"This guy's walking around like Barney Fife and someone in the back is letting him have it with the Richard Pryor tape," Billings said. "I was really digging it."

Eventually, forms were filled out, the van returned with pancakes for the team, a front-end loader arrived to load the horse carcasses into a dump truck, and at 6 a.m. a new bus showed up to complete the trip to Dover. As they made the last two hours of the drive, Purzycki thought about the incident. At a moment when they had just survived a harrowing ordeal, a cop had referred to his players as "colored," differentiated people by skin color, and treated them as if they were the problem. Purzycki couldn't decide if the guy was ignorant, callous, a racist, or all of the above.

His three years at Delaware State gave him a unique perspective for a white man. He could honestly say he knew what it was like to be a minority. But what he had just been through reinforced his belief that he'd never know what it was like to be black.

TWENTY-EIGHT

When he attended the MEAC pre-season football coaches' meetings in 1981 there were people who wouldn't speak to Purzycki. That tension was extended onto the field by a few coaches in 1981 and 1982. By the start of the 1983 season, his presence at Delaware State had been accepted by most and those who worried about negative ramifications that could develop from a white head coach at an HBCU were much fewer and less vocal.

By the end of the 1983 season, the transformation was complete: the league's coaches thought enough of him and the job he had done to name him the MEAC Coach of the Year.

He was also named the MEAC Coach of the Year by the Pigskin Club of Washington D.C., an organization formed in 1938 by Charles Fisher. Dr. Fisher played football at Howard and conceived of the organization to honor great achievement in black college football.

Purzycki joined a list of heavyweights to have received recognition from the Pigskin Club. Past honorees included Eddie Robinson of Grambling (408 wins and nine national titles), Clarence "Big House" Gaines of Winston-Salem State (who coached football for three years in the 1940s before focusing on a basketball coaching career that landed him into the Naismith Memorial Basketball Hall of Fame), Jake Gaither of Florida A&M (who won 204 games and six national titles), and Willie Jeffries of South Carolina State (who won back-to-back national titles before being hired by Wichita State in 1979, becoming the first black head coach in Division I college football).

"Both awards meant a great deal to me," Purzycki said. "The award from the conference came from my peers and it's always special to be recognized in that way. The Pigskin Club had so much history and prestige, and to be honored by them was humbling."

He didn't speak at the MEAC ceremony but was asked to give a short speech by the Pigskin Club. In the speech, he recognized some of the past honorees and talked of how great it felt to be mentioned in that same group. He also praised the people in the black college football community and at Delaware State who had been supportive. It had been easy in the early days to focus on the detractors. At times, it had been impossible *not* to focus on them. Purzycki had felt in his heart that those who had been with him outnumbered those who had been against him. He could see that clearly now.

He wasn't the only one who had a different view of things. At a postseason banquet in Dover, DSC president Luna Mishoe introduced Purzycki by asking the crowd to "give it up for *my* football coach, Joe Purzycki."

At a nearby table, Diane Townsend turned to her husband with wide eyes and said quietly, "I thought he was *your* football coach."

Nelson reached under the table and squeezed her hand and they both smiled. Among Townsend's list of qualities was an utter lack of concern over who got credit for success. He believed it was athletes who deserved most of it, anyway, and he wasn't going to get too hung up on Dr. Mishoe's sudden change from *your* to *my*.

Dr. Mishoe was likely just making an inside joke for the benefit of Townsend. The president had certainly reminded him on occasion that Purzycki was all Townsend's idea, but he also had backed Townsend and the decision to hire Purzycki publicly despite the massive negative reaction. He stayed firmly behind the duo during the tough times in 1981 and '82, and despite not agreeing with Townsend's choice initially he never pressured the AD to make a change, ultimately allowing him to see his vision through.

Purzycki didn't concern himself with it, either. He had inadvertently created some problems with *his* head coach and needed to spend some time during the off-season patching up his relationship with Tubby Raymond.

After all, 1983 was not Raymond's best year. The Blue Hens 4-and-7 record was one of only four seasons in his 35 years as Delaware head coach that his team had a losing season. While this was happening, his protégé, the guy he had advised against taking the Delaware State job, was enjoying a breakout year and the accolades that came with it.

Raymond didn't wish Purzycki ill will and was happy for his success. But it seemed to him as if every Sunday morning there was a picture of Purzycki on the front page of the sports section celebrating another win next to a picture of Raymond and his players trying to explain another setback. Exacerbating things was an issue that worked its way under his skin as his team struggled through 1983.

In 1978, Delaware and Delaware State reached a tentative agreement for the schools to meet in a two-year football series in 1983 and 1984. The agreement was endorsed by fans, alums, players, and the presidents of both schools. Then, Delaware backed out, saying it wanted to add Bucknell to the schedule, instead.

In a 1982 story in the *News Journal*, Townsend (who was hired at Del State in 1979) said, "Every year I've been the AD at Delaware State" he had proposed a game between the two schools. "It appears to me it is just a matter of policy at Delaware. I'm not so sure it is Dave Nelson's philosophy, but the institution has decided it is not wise to play their little sister institution in Delaware."

By pointing out that he didn't think this was UD athletic director Dave Nelson's philosophy, Townsend opened the door for speculation about whose policy it was to not play Del State. That speculation landed squarely (and accurately) on Raymond.

Raymond felt the Blue Hens had nothing to gain by playing Delaware State. If they won, they were only doing what they were supposed to do. They were a national powerhouse, after all. If they lost, the embarrassment would be too much to stand. That possibility, minute as it was when the agreement was reached and then broken, meant the risk outweighed the reward.

Purzycki was still an assistant coach for Raymond when the Blue Hens backed out of the deal. Five years later he was in Dover leading the resurgence of the Del State program. Raymond had not seen any of that coming, and as his 1983 season wore on, he was thankful that he had insisted on not scheduling Delaware State for a game that season.

"When we became good in 1983 there was a real clamoring for the game," Purzycki said. "In speeches, and in the media, I began comparing the two programs, since I was in the unique position of knowing both of them intimately. I constantly pointed out that we were achieving success without a big stadium, with a fraction of Delaware's recruiting budget, and with no history of success."

One of Purzycki's go-to lines in speeches he made to promote his program involved his first-year recruiting budget ($300) and his first-year recruiting class (10 players).

"I like to tell my guys that they cost me thirty bucks apiece," he'd tell laughing crowds of fans at various clubs and athletic organizations around Delaware. People ate it up. Purzycki had always been popular in the state, first as an All-American at UD, then as a state championship-winning coach at Caesar Rodney High School, and finally as the coach of a plucky underdog beginning to have success. He was funny, great with the media, and now was winning games and often wondering aloud why Delaware didn't want to play Delaware State.

Raymond began to feel as if the knife was being stuck in him a little too often and a little too deep. He was having a down year, sure, but he also had taken the Blue Hens to the postseason 11 times. It irritated him that people insinuated he was scared to play Delaware State and at his speeches to the same clubs Purzycki was talking to, he began reminding people that everything Purzycki (and several guys on his staff) knew about football had been learned at Delaware.

He also said that Del State's one year of success was great but pointed out that the success he enjoyed at Delaware had been a long-term thing and he was, "not planning on being run out of the state."

Inevitably, there came a night when Purzycki and Raymond were at the same banquet. That night, the mentor made a point of saying how proud he was for Purzycki's success at Del State and that he thought there was more than enough room in Delaware for two successful Division I-AA programs. The two spoke after the banquet and agreed to do a better job communicating directly rather than through the media.

But the media loved the story and wouldn't leave it alone. In their preview section for the 1984 season, the *News Journal* ran a story under the headline "Tubby and Joe leave ruffled feathers behind" that detailed the rift that had developed between the two men in 1983.

"For a while last season," Purzycki told reporter Gene Bryson, "I was so pleased with the prospect of where we were going that I might have said some things about their program that I shouldn't have. It certainly wasn't a conscious thing on my part to attack them. It was unwitting because I still feel like a part of their family, but I said some things I shouldn't have, and it ruffled some feathers...some Hen feathers. But I think Tubby knows me well enough to know my intentions. I was trying to help my program, not hurt his."

Raymond downplayed the entire kerfuffle. "There were maybe a couple of statements made that maybe were taken wrong," he said. Asked by Bryson about tension between the two, the Blue Hens' boss insisted the issue was moot.

"There are no bad feelings whatsoever," Raymond insisted to Bryson. "What happened last year goes with the flow of things. We happened to be down, and Del State happened to be up. But to say I was disturbed by what Delaware State did is way out of line."

Raymond later told Purzycki that he hated Bryson's story and didn't like this kind of business being played out in the newspaper. Purzycki pointed out that the story wasn't *his* idea and he simply answered Bryson's questions. Unlike Raymond, he loved the story.

"We both got over it. But, as far as I was concerned, the more people who were willing to talk about us, the better," Purzycki said. "It was positive for us. For people to talk about Delaware and Delaware State in the same sentence ... our alums and supporters loved it."

His athletic director did, too.

"Nelson derived tremendous pleasure from the entire thing. He loved the comparisons," Purzycki added. "There had been plenty of disparaging remarks about Delaware State athletics in the newspapers over the years. He knew that for us to be in the same conversation as Delaware was a good thing."

It had been, after all, a primary reason he had hired Purzycki in the first place.

TWENTY-NINE

Nelson Townsend stood in a Philadelphia hotel lobby feeling the mixture of pride and satisfaction.

The plan had worked.

He exchanged greetings and accepted congratulations from a long line of fans and alums decked out in Delaware State colors, most of whom probably couldn't believe the weekend they were having.

Delaware State had defeated South Carolina State, 50-36, in front of more than 12,000 fans in the inaugural "Football Classic" at Philadelphia's Franklin Field. The game was the 1984 season-opener for both schools and served as the centerpiece of a weekend-long celebration that included a $100-a-plate dinner the night before the game, with Dr. Luna Mishoe as the guest of honor. After the game, fans stayed in Philadelphia Saturday night to celebrate the big victory at a DSC dance.

Townsend had conceived of the idea during the 1983 season when the Hornets first began having success under Purzycki. Since the 1920s, HBCUs around the country had staged so-called classic games as a way to celebrate their football programs: take a game already on the schedule, play it at a neutral site, and use the game to increase interest and exposure for the schools involved. For Delaware State, it was another chance to be mentioned with the big-time programs in black college football.

"Our football program has developed somewhat over the past few years," Townsend said to *News Journal* columnist Jack Chevalier two days before the game. "This is something new to Delaware State. We're trying to establish a new tradition."

Townsend's direct boss at DSC was vice president for student affairs Dr. Gladys Motley. She had been supportive of Townsend and Purzycki from day one and was an enthusiastic backer of the idea that Delaware State play in this type of game.

"I attended a Morgan State-Grambling State game in New York when I was young," she told Chevalier, "and I really enjoyed the camaraderie. Just being there meeting all the people was a special occasion."

Townsend and Purzycki had received an indication of how special the occasion could feel the night before the game. Purzycki was on his way into a banquet room to talk to his team when he noticed Townsend staring out a window in a common area of the hotel.

"We usually stayed at motels, but for this game, we were booked into a big-time hotel in the center of Philadelphia," Purzycki said. "I walked over to him and asked him what he was doing."

"Look," was Townsend's one-word reply.

Purzycki followed Townsend's gaze out the window and found himself looking at the Philadelphia Electric Company building, known by locals as the PECO Building. A prominent feature of the City of Brotherly Love's skyline, it has a huge electronic display board on top that shows time, temperature, and other messages. He watched as the lights flashed their message:

"The Football Classic," crawled across the board. "Kickoff 1:00 p.m. Saturday at Franklin Field. The Delaware State Hornets vs. the South Carolina State Bulldogs."

"I'll never forget it," Purzycki said. "We looked at each other with big smiles on our faces and a contentment that came from a journey only the two of us really understood."

Purzycki scrapped whatever plans he had for that night's speech to his team and instead gave a brief accounting on where Del State had been, where they were now, and how hard they had all worked to get there.

"Who would have thought that we'd be at historic Franklin Field one day," he asked his team, "playing one of the best HBCU programs in the country, and with our name in lights above the great city of Philadelphia the night before the game?"

The idea to play the game at Franklin Field was enthusiastically received by fans and students who filled 25 buses in Dover and another

10 in Wilmington. Between transportation, renting Franklin Field, the Friday dinner, and the Saturday night dance, the game became the most ambitious undertaking in Delaware State athletics history.

"I was in awe of everything that was happening," Purzycki admitted. "I was a little worried about how our team would react. But we were the favorite. And we went out and did what the favorite is supposed to do. We won big."

Back at the hotel after the game, Townsend continued the celebration with happy fans.

"This was a special day for Delaware State," he said to the *News Journal*. "We had the excitement of the crowd and the game itself. Everything here went pretty much as we have planned. This is a highlight for our program. This day is just about what we've worked for over the years."

As Townsend smiled and laughed and greeted friends, he eventually noticed Herky Billings standing in the hotel's cigar shop. He walked over and shook Billings' hand in congratulations.

"What are you looking for?" he asked.

"I'm looking for a damn good cigar to smoke after that win," Billings said with a laugh.

"You pick whatever one you want," Townsend said to the coach whose offense had piled up 523 yards and 50 points against the perennial best team in the MEAC. "It's on me."

The stogie was the first of many celebratory ones burned in 1984 as the Hornets rolled to an eight-win season. As in 1983, they had success early, a dip in the middle, and a strong finish.

They primarily rode the talented legs of Gene Lake who established school records that still stand for total rushing yards in a season (1,722), rushing yards in a game (336 against Liberty), touchdowns in a season (20), touchdowns in a game (six) against Howard, and career touchdowns (35). Lake was named an All-American and selected as the Delaware athlete of the year by writers and broadcasters. His career total of 3,123 yards rushing (in just two seasons) ranks among the best in MEAC history.

As a team, the 1984 Hornets rushed for an average of 377 yards a game, which was more than any school in any division in college football.

John Taylor set school records with 758 yards receiving and 10 touchdowns, and Pat Spencer's 1,317 yards passing were another DSC mark.

Bill Collick's defense gave up just 93 points in the Hornets' eight wins, including five games with a touchdown or less. After South Carolina State scored 36 in the season opener, Collick's crew threw a shutout at Northeastern (35-0) and gave up only a late first-half touchdown against North Carolina A&T (56-7).

"You realize some things that go on when you're getting your brains beat out," Collick said. "By 1984, I felt good about our defense. Teams weren't going to take the ball and shove it down our throats anymore. We were getting better."

The Hornets were 3-and-0 after that win and were ranked 7th in the country. But they dropped a pair of road games – 41-38 at Bethune-Cookman and 20-19 at James Madison.

The loss to Bethune-Cookman was frustrating because the Hornets turned the ball over seven times in a game they felt they let get away. The loss to James Madison was maddening because the Hornets outplayed the Dukes all day and felt the game was taken from them by the officials.

"I can say, without question, this was the worst group of officials I've ever witnessed on a football field," the fiery Purzycki said after the defeat. "They were bad for either team and they had a direct bearing on the game, and that should never happen."

Del State led the game 7-6 at halftime. Purzycki was irritated about a penalty that led to JMU's first field goal and incensed about a penalty that led to their second one. Late in the first quarter, JMU kicker Mickey Stinnett missed a 51-yard field goal attempt. He was given a second chance after Del State was whistled for being offside on the play. The Hornets linemen all claimed a JMU player had moved before the snap, but the call stood in favor of the Dukes and given a second chance, Stinnett banged home a 46-yard attempt.

Then, late in the half, JMU elected to go for it on fourth-and-one. Defensive tackle Dan Candeloro stuffed the play and Delaware State had the ball. As one official came in to reset and mark the ball for the Hornets possession, another official lobbed in a penalty flag. After a conference, the officials (an all-white crew from the Division III Old

Dominion Athletic Conference) announced that JMU had been called for delay of game. Instead of Del State getting the football, the Dukes were penalized five yards, but they would now have another chance at a fourth down play. Stinnett quickly connected on a 48-yard field goal.

"On that day, it felt like calls were going against us because we were a black college," said Candeloro (who is white).

"They cheated us the whole game," John Taylor said. "They kept calling penalties against jersey numbers we didn't have. It was unbelievable."

The delay of game whistled well after the play was the final bit of heat that caused Purzycki's personal pot to boil over. At halftime, as the officials jogged to their locker room, they had Purzycki as a wingman verbally blasting them and the nine penalties they had called on his team in the first 30 minutes.

"It's the worst I ever saw him yell," Candeloro said. "He really unloaded on those guys."

"We were getting cheated," said defensive tackle Joe Lane. "We were all mad. I remember the assistants were holding him back. He went after them with everything he had."

"That last call was complete bullshit," Purzycki yelled at the officials. "Delay of game, *after* we had stopped them? It's a bullshit call. Why are you throwing so many flags on us and not on them? Why are you doing this to us? Is it because *we're* black?"

The officials entered their locker room and Purzycki had no choice but to turn and go towards his. That's when he first noticed Townsend who had jogged off the field just behind Purzycki. He was afraid his coach was going to get tossed out of the game and he wanted to be there to try and prevent it. He had watched enough football to know a hosing when he was seeing one and he agreed with his coach that the deck seemed stacked against the road team in this game.

He was also quite possibly the only person on Earth who could say something to Purzycki in the heat of this particular moment. He smiled as he approached his coach: "Is it because '*We're* black?'" he deadpanned. "*Really?*"

The second half wasn't as flag-filled as the first, and the two teams exchanged the lead three times. JMU won 20-19 when DSC was unable to convert a two-point conversion after their final touchdown.

Del State outgained JMU 470 yards to 300 and had the football for nearly 37 minutes. They sacked JMU's quarterback four times and intercepted two passes and recovered two fumbles ... and lost.

"Things didn't go our way," Lane told the *News Journal*, "but that wasn't because of us. They were caused by others and those were things we couldn't control."

Similar to 1983, the Hornets bounced back from their two-game slide and finished the year on a winning streak. That included a 70-8 rout of Bowie State that brought back some interesting memories for offensive tackle Matt Horace. He was enjoying a fifth year at Del State because of an injury suffered early in the 1983 season. He was the last player with the program who had been at Civic Stadium in Portland on that wretched night in 1980 when Portland State had humiliated Del State, 105-0.

"I've never forgotten that night," Horace told Gene Bryson of the *News Journal*. "Back then, people would look at our football players and laugh. They'd say we were nothing. But I'm proud I stayed with it here. I'm proud this program has gotten to where it is."

They followed up with a win over Towson State, a homecoming rout of Central State, and easy wins over Howard and Liberty to finish the year 8-2, on a five-game winning streak. The day before the Central State game, Luna Mishoe hosted the team at a luncheon. There, he introduced the Hornets to William Granville, Delaware State College Class of 1962.

Granville was the vice president of Mobil Oil Company and he was one of 23 DSC alumni who had joined together to form a group Dr. Mishoe called "The Delaware State Connection" whose goal was to support the program financially and help players find jobs following their playing careers. Like the playing of the "Football Classic" that started the season in Philadelphia, the formation of "The Delaware State Connection" was an idea that could not have been conceived with a straight face just a few years earlier.

Townsend's gamble on Purzycki had paid off. On the night he was hired, Purzycki had shared with the school's leaders his vision for the program. They would concentrate on recruiting local and regional players to build interest in the program. They would help those players academically to ensure they stayed in school and could become successful students and experienced football players.

The oft-referenced "2-4-6-8" plan had also worked. Purzycki said there would be limited success on the field for the first two years and then delivered on the promised payoff with back-to-back winning seasons. The team had even achieved the honor of a national ranking for several weeks in both 1983 and 1984. By the end of 1984, Delaware State football was in a place of success few could have imagined in 1981.

They also were looking for a new head coach.

Purzycki had been honest with DSC officials and the media from the day he was hired. He was grateful for the job, looked forward to the challenge, but he was young and had lots of ambition. If he had success at Del State it was inevitable other schools would pursue him. He had been linked to the Villanova job in 1983, but he felt he still had work to do in Dover. By the conclusion of the 1984 season, he had delivered on every promise he had made to Delaware State.

"Nelson and I had long talks from the very beginning about my long-term career goals," Purzycki said. "He knew I wanted to be a Division I coach, and that I likely couldn't get that kind of a job from Delaware State. We both knew there was going to have to be another stop."

Townsend agreed with Purzycki that it would be tough to jump from Del State to Division I and he used to tell him he knew the day was coming when Purzycki would leave Dover. Townsend had actually discussed that idea with his coach and had told him several times that he had a plan for when Purzycki left.

"We're an HBCU, and you were brought here to do a specific job: to build a program and get it moving in the right direction," Townsend said to Purzycki. "You were the best man for that job, but when you leave, I think it's going to be better to come back to our historic roots. Delaware State provides a wonderful opportunity for so many students and I think it's important that we also provide as many examples as we can of strong African American role models. That should include the football coach."

"It's another example of how good his vision was," Purzycki said. "He thought I was the right guy for the job in 1981 because he needed to make a radical change. He needed a coach who could win back the community and he knew that just up the road was a program that had won five national championships and was the gold standard for I-AA football. He got all that when he hired me.

"But even before we started having success, he was already thinking about his next move, why he would do it, and what it would mean. He was a brilliant guy."

In December, Purzycki informed Townsend that he was talking to officials from James Madison University about the Dukes' vacant football job. They had a bigger stadium, more money in the budget, and an ambitious plan to grow the football program. If Purzycki took the job and had success, JMU could better serve as a launching pad to a Division I job. By December 19th, he had reached an agreement with JMU. That's when Luna Mishoe entered the picture.

"Dr. Mishoe called me at my house that night," Purzycki said. "He told me that the school wanted me to stay and had put together an offer that was $5,000 higher than what JMU was going to pay me."

Purzycki was flattered and even wavered a little on his decision. But in the end, money wasn't the primary reason he was taking the JMU job. He was young, ambitious, and felt it would better fit his career goals.

"For my professional goals," he told DSC's president, "I think I have to take this job." Mishoe was disappointed, but like Townsend, he understood and wished him well. Five days before Christmas, Purzycki accepted an offer to be the head coach at James Madison University in Harrisonburg, Virginia.

"You were the Grinch who stole our Christmas," Townsend told him with a laugh.

THIRTY

Nelson Townsend was nearing his wit's end. For the second time in four years, he was tasked with hiring a football coach at Delaware State College. And for the second time in four years, that job was proving much more difficult than he thought it should be.

On the day Purzycki turned in his resignation (December 20, 1984), Townsend was ready. As in 1981, he had identified his top choice for the job quickly, but this time there wouldn't be a lot of outside noise and controversy. Townsend felt there was an obvious way to go. He was so certain, he expected to have his new coach in place and recruiting for Delaware State by the end of the day.

Then, Bill Collick turned him down.

When Purzycki resigned Townsend immediately met with Collick, Herky Billings, Jeff Cannon, and Greg McLaurin and assured each that he would be considered for the head job. Billings, Cannon, and McLaurin all told the athletic director that they were committed to Purzycki and had accepted jobs with him at JMU. But Collick indicated he'd be interested in discussing the situation at Delaware State further, and within two hours of Purzycki's resignation, Townsend offered him the job.

What should have been a done deal got muddied up due to a couple of things. First, Collick was obviously plugged in around the DSC campus and had heard rumors that while Townsend indeed wanted him as the new head coach, there were others who weren't so sure.

"Nelson knew what he wanted," Collick said. "He wanted me to take the job. But I heard he had to sell me to some of the other people on campus and I wasn't sure how serious the offer was."

Collick had never been a head football coach. And even though he had heard rumblings of Purzycki's possible departure, everything happened so swiftly that he was left unsure of what to think.

He also had Purzycki in his ear, urging him to follow the rest of the staff to Harrisonburg. The last four years had been the most fun of his professional career and it was tempting to think they could recreate that kind of feeling at another school. But moving to Virginia ran counter to Collick's personality. He was born, raised, and had lived his entire life in Delaware. He was only 32 and he loved coaching, but he had already decided he wasn't going to be the kind of guy who moved around the country just to coach football.

Yet, JMU wasn't that far away, Purzycki's charisma was hard to say no to, and he was unsure how many people (other than Townsend) wanted him to stay in Dover. So, he packed up and headed to the Shenandoah Valley.

Townsend was disappointed but quickly moved on to the next name on his list, a guy familiar to everyone at DSC.

Billy Joe had been the focus of so much interest in 1981. Three days after Purzycki was given the job, Joe and the Eagles lost to Oakland in Super Bowl XV. Shortly after that, he'd taken the job at Central State in Ohio where he'd rolled up a 32-and-14 record that included two trips to the Division II playoffs.

In early January, with rumors of an offer forthcoming from Del State, Joe announced his intention to remain at Central State. (He stayed at the Ohio school until 1993 piling up 12 consecutive winning seasons and 11 consecutive trips to the playoffs. He was hired as the head coach at Florida A&M in 1993.)

With Collick settling in at JMU and Joe staying at Central State, DSC turned its attention to Bill Hayes, who was the head coach at Winston-Salem State. In nine seasons with the Rams, he had an impressive 64-31-2 record. Hayes said that he liked the situation at Del State and would think long and hard about accepting an offer to coach there. DSC made Hayes an offer a few days later only to be rebuffed again when Hayes declined.

An exasperated Townsend knew what he wanted to do next. He wanted his first, best option to come through, after all. He'd heard rumors that Collick was already homesick in Virginia. He had been the guy Townsend wanted for the job since the moment Purzycki handed him a letter of resignation. After conferring with Mishoe ("Call him back and tell him we're still interested in him," the president told him) Townsend put in a call to Collick's house in Delaware. His wife Nancy answered.

"Will you talk to Bill sometime today?" Townsend asked.

"Yes," Nancy Collick responded. "We talk every night."

"When you do," Townsend said, "tell him Dr. Mishoe and I are still very interested in hiring him as the next football coach at Delaware State. We'd like to speak to him as soon as possible. Will you do that for me? Will you tell him that tonight when you speak to him?"

Nancy Collick had been opposed to leaving Delaware in the first place. She had a good job, they had just had their second child, and she wanted to raise the kids around their grandmothers who both lived nearby.

"Nelson, I'm not going to tell him that tonight," she said. "I'm going to tell him that right now. Because as soon as I get off the phone with you, I'm calling Bill."

Within a couple of days, Bill Collick was introduced as Joe Purzycki's successor at Delaware State. Like Purzycki, he had various apprehensions about taking the job. And like Purzycki, he turned to Townsend for guidance.

"He treated me a like a son," Collick said. "He'd kick me when I needed it. When he saw something he didn't like he let me know it. But he also hugged me when I needed it. He really wanted me to be the coach and he thought I could do it. He didn't have a lot of support for me (from others on campus) at first, but he had a lot of faith in me and I felt that.

"There were high expectations for whoever came in after Joe, and Nelson trusted me with the job," Collick said. "He always told me he was depending on me."

Collick had earned Townsend's admiration during Purzycki's first two tumultuous years in Dover when he had remained loyal both to the head coach and to what they were all trying to accomplish.

"Nelson appreciated how trustworthy Bill had become," Diane Townsend said. "He knew how some people felt and he could have talked against Joe in an effort to take over the situation, but he was not that kind of man."

"If he could work with someone under the conditions they worked," Townsend said to his wife, "he can be trusted. And a man like that can be a winner."

"Nelson knew we had spent four years building that program, using that offense and that defense," Purzycki said. "He knew that it was important at this point to have continuity, but he had to convince everybody that despite his lack of head coaching experience Bill could do the job. Nelson had that vision for Bill's future and as we came to find out, he was right."

Collick had some of Purzycki's qualities but had a distinctly different personality. They both had football knowledge, a deep competitive streak, and a passion for organization. But where Purzycki's passion was fueled by an inner fire that sometimes flared out of control, Collick's was more like a stovetop burner, measured and consistent.

"I can remember being so angry about something at halftime one game," Purzycki laughed, "that I was throwing cans of soda at guys. They were running and hiding. Then Bill stepped in. 'OK, guys. We've got to get our composure back.'"

"Coach Purzycki would see a building on fire, and he would run right in," Joe Lane said. "Coach Collick would call the fire department. Collick would do and say a lot of the same things Purzycki did, he'd just do and say them in a different way."

During a game in 1984 defensive lineman Dan Candeloro drew three penalties on one play, the last one for throwing his helmet in disgust at the first two calls. The staff knew Candeloro had huge talent, but they were always working with him to channel his emotion properly. As he came to the sideline after his helmet toss Purzycki leveled him with a verbal blast. Then, as he sat on the bench still stewing, Collick approached him.

"Dan," Collick said, "when you've got it made in the shade, you can't keep letting trees fall on your head."

Greg McLaurin had gone to JMU with Purzycki but came back to Dover when Collick made him his defensive coordinator. He said that when he first joined Purzycki's DSC staff in 1981 he couldn't figure Collick out.

"At first I wondered why he was a college football coach," McLaurin said. "On road trips, when the rest of us would try to find a high school game to watch, he'd take a walk around town and maybe shop at an antique store. He loved football, but at times it was the furthest thing from his mind."

But the more he was around him, the more he appreciated and came to understand Collick's approach to coaching.

"He was so patient, and nothing rattled him. Guys would go off and get into trouble and people would be ready to condemn them and Bill would always wait until he had the full story. He always took his time with problems and gave players the benefit of the doubt. We nicknamed him 'Job.'"

Collick also had achieved something that no coach in Delaware State athletic history had done. In addition to his assistant coaching duties under Purzycki, he was DSC's wrestling coach and in 1984 his wrestling team won the school's first-ever MEAC championship.

"That was big," McLaurin said. "That created a positive atmosphere around the football team. If *they* can do it, *we* can do it."

As he began stacking up days on the job, Collick realized that both Purzycki and Townsend had prepared him well for this opportunity. He had arrived at Del State in 1981 at the age of 28 with just four years as a high school assistant under his belt. During his time as Purzycki's defensive coordinator, he was gradually given more responsibilities by both his coach and his athletic director.

"Joe knew the players needed someone close to them saying things to them that he couldn't say to them," Diane Townsend said. "In other words, he needed somebody black. That was very insightful, and he gave Bill that role and that responsibility because he knew he could trust him to build that relationship and not worry about him taking over or confusing the players as to who was in charge.

"Without even knowing it, his role was extended. He became a guy who the players talked to about life. It wasn't that they couldn't talk to Purzycki. But many of them had no experience talking to anybody white about certain things about their lives and their families."

"Each season, Nelson and Joe would add a little more to my job," Collick said. "It was an unbelievable time when I look at the growth for me as a person. I was doing the administrative work, booking plane flights, setting up meals. If you make a mistake there, it's glaring. I began to realize that I had done more to get ready to be a head coach than I thought. Once I got there, I really believed I could do it and do it successfully."

Collick used his calm demeanor in the same effective manner in which Purzycki had channeled his often-manic energy. Collick's philosophy was centered on the idea that if you create a calm, efficient, in-control attitude, your team will reflect that and maintain their composure during difficult times.

"Bill became a better head football coach than me," Purzycki said. "He had the perfect disposition, He never got too high and never got too low and that allowed his teams to stay on a steady line. He was a wonderful recruiter, he ended up like a father figure to most of his guys."

Collick was able to take advantage of one situation that Purzycki had to earn. He was a very popular hire with the players and enjoyed almost unconditional support within the team. And despite his concerns that some people on campus had to be convinced he was the right man for the job, his power base from the beginning was deep and wide.

"There were a lot of people there who did not want me to fail," he said. "And after what we had accomplished in '83 and '84, there were a lot of people all over Delaware who wanted us to succeed. We had become a place where Delaware kids could get an education, play in a winning football program, and be close enough to home their families could watch them play. That was a big part of our success."

The players were on-board from day one. Candeloro, who would blossom into an All-American defensive lineman under Collick, had arrived at DSC in 1982. He was one of just a few white players on the team and says he never had a problem with any of his teammates in terms of that. Still, it was a foreign atmosphere at first and he remembered the person who helped him figure out those early tentative days.

"One of the first days I was there I walked into study hall and I was apprehensive," he said. "Coach Collick was there and talked to me right away. He asked me if I was going to be OK. From that day on, he was the guy I talked to the most. He was always there for me."

As for people who weren't in Collick's camp? "I took little heed to anyone who was a naysayer," Collick said. He also did one big thing his first year on the job that helped immensely: He won.

The 1985 Hornets went 9-2. They beat Morgan State 35-0. They beat Bethune-Cookman 51-7. Southern fell 46-8. Northeastern 36-6. John Taylor caught five passes for 223 yards and three touchdowns in a 46-6 rout of St. Paul's. DSC went unbeaten in MEAC play to win its first conference championship.

"Bill told me later that we should have given MEAC rings to Purzycki, Billings, and Cannon," McLaurin said, "because they had a lot to do with the success we had in 1985."

That season continued a run of success that's never been duplicated at Delaware State and hasn't happened at too many other places. Between Purzycki's final two seasons and Collick's first 11, the Hornets posted 13 consecutive winning seasons.

Collick's run at the school was a huge success by any measure and he remains the winningest coach in Del State football history. The only negative to his time in Dover was the lack of an invitation to the Division I-AA playoffs. On a couple of occasions, they were on the doorstep before late-season losses crushed their chances. And in his first season, they were done in by a confounding bureaucratic dispute within the MEAC that impacted Delaware State in two ways.

Florida A&M left the MEAC before the 1984 season in a disagreement over the future of their rivalry game with fellow conference member Bethune-Cookman. The league wanted to stage the game in an annual "classic" format and play it at a neutral field in Tampa. Mindful of their powerful home-field advantage, the Rattlers balked at the idea and when pressed, elected to strike out as an independent.

Their departure meant the MEAC didn't have enough teams to gain an automatic berth into the playoffs in 1985, which left Collick's first team hoping to make the field as an at-large team. Their ranking and performance indicated that was a strong possibility, but they were snubbed by the playoff committee despite a 9-and-2 record and a No. 12 ranking in the polls.

FAMU's departure from the league impacted Delaware State a second way a few months after the season. Their two-year run as an independent was disastrous and the athletic department was filled with acrimony between those who had been in favor of leaving the MEAC and those who had wanted to stay. Scheduling as an independent had been a nightmare and the rare (by FAMU standards) back-to-back losing seasons left fans and alums grumbling. Athletic Director Roosevelt Wilson resigned under pressure. Coach Rudy Hubbard was fired.

By 1986, Florida A&M wanted back in the MEAC. The school needed to find someone to guide them through that transition with a firm hand while also possessing the patience and wisdom to repair fractured relationships on campus.

In February of 1986, Florida A&M hired Nelson Townsend as their new athletic director. He would stay there for two years and assimilate them back into the MEAC before taking the same job at the University of Buffalo, where his 12-year run included an ambitious and successful four-year plan to move the Bulls athletic teams from Division III to Division I.

Collick, meanwhile, remained at Delaware State under new athletic director John Martin ... and just kept winning.

"We continued to be successful at recruiting," Collick said, "but we also had gotten to the point where we were good enough that kids were starting to come to us. That was a big moment."

His teams went 25-and-7 during his first three seasons and an event that triggered a spontaneous celebration for Purzycki and Townsend when it first happened in 1983 now became routine: The Hornets spent 25 weeks ranked in the Division I-AA top 20 poll.

After a .500 year in 1988, they went 23-and-9 over the next three seasons and picked up several signature wins (including a rout of Division I Akron and a win in Dover over eventual national champ Youngstown State). In his first seven seasons, Collick's teams went 30-and-8 in the MEAC, winning the conference title outright four times and grabbing a co-championship another time. Bad luck and circumstances conspired to keep them out of the playoffs, but the program was generally acknowledged among the best in Division I-AA football.

Factor in Purzycki's final two years, and in the nine seasons between 1983 and 1991 Delaware State was 68-26-1 (a .721 winning percentage). No other MEAC team won more than 50 games during the same period. Delaware won 63 games. Grambling won 66 times. Speaking of Grambling...

With all the success it was not a surprise when Delaware State was offered a slot as the Tigers' opponent in the first Motor City Classic at Detroit's Pontiac Silverdome in 1992.

"Things that we had once only dreamed about were happening," Collick said. "We had moved the program that far forward."

THIRTY-ONE

Collick could be forgiven if he was a little overwhelmed at the opportunity to match football wits against Grambling coach Eddie Robinson.

Collick entered the Pontiac Silverdome with 55 career wins. Robinson had 373. Collick became a head coach in 1985. Robinson became a head coach in 1941 – 11 years before Collick was born. Robinson had long been a hero within the black college football coaching fraternity and a legend in the sport, and Collick was still in the process of making his own name.

"It was hard to believe I had come all the way from being an assistant coach at Cape Henlopen High School to going against this guy," Collick recalled. "He had done so much for so many for so long. It was intimidating. But in a good way."

Collick got a nice little assist a few days before the game when one of the event's organizers called him and advised him to take the first of two practice time slots allocated at the Silverdome the day before the game.

"Coach, you've got to practice first," he was told. "Because if you let Coach Robinson practice first, he'll take all his time, then he'll take all your time, and because he's Coach Robinson, no one will say anything to him."

Intimidating. In a good way. That's what happens when you have the kind of success Robinson had at Grambling. Collick thought his team would be like him: maybe a little wide-eyed, but certainly ready to step onto the big stage and mix it up.

"Our team knew about Grambling's mystique and their tradition, but we had been good for a long while and I did not expect us to be in awe of them," he said. "We had gotten to the point where we expected to win games like this."

"We had always been willing to play anyone," McLaurin said. "To us, Grambling was another opportunity to get a notch on our belt. I knew we'd be ready."

Herky Billings agreed with Collick and McLaurin. Billings had returned to Delaware State in 1991 after things didn't work out at James Madison. With the Hornets again, he picked up where he left off producing an offense that was always among the best running teams in the country. He looked forward to the Motor City Classic and thought the Hornets could handle the attendant noise of the event. He wasn't worried about much of anything until the first time he set eyes on the Tigers.

"Grambling was warming up and I went out to take a look at them," Billings said. "My first reaction was that (Del State athletic director) John Martin should be fired. I remember thinking to myself, 'What are we doing playing these guys? This is insane.' I felt like their third-team guys in warmups looked bigger and stronger than us."

A crowd estimated at over 26,000 settled in likely feeling the same way. The Hornets were better than they once were, but this was Grambling and in every possible pre-game comparison, the Tigers looked superior to the Hornets. Both school's bands performed before the game and by kickoff, the crowd was roaring and ready for a game.

Boy, did they get one.

In a wild evening on the Silverdome carpet, the two teams combined for 87 points and nearly 1,000 total yards. Del State led at halftime 20-14, but a trio of Grambling scores gave the Tigers a 35-20 lead late in the third quarter. The deficit was not overly daunting for DSC because Collick's teams had built a reputation as comeback artists. In previous seasons, they had come from 21 down to beat Bethune-Cookman and from 28 back to beat Liberty. Many of the players in Detroit had played in those games.

"The kids on the sidelines kept saying, 'Remember Liberty! Remember Liberty!'" Collick said. "They never felt like we were out of the game."

Down 15, the Hornets dug into their bag of tricks to keep a drive alive. During the week, special teams coach Andre Williams had noticed that Grambling took a lot of time getting players on and off the field. He felt the Tigers might be susceptible to a fake punt at some point during the game. Collick agreed but wanted nothing left to chance. Fullback Darald Stancil was the personal protector for the punter and stood a few yards in front of him. It would be up to him to determine if the play would work and Collick had been telling him all week that if he called for the play Stancil had better get the first down. When they got ready to use the fake in the game, Collick reminded him again.

"We're going to call it," he told Stancil, "but you better get the first down. You've got a big problem with me if you don't get the damn thing."

Delaware State lined up to punt, Grambling was a touch slow getting guys on the field, and Stancil called for the fake. He took the snap, ran to his left, and the entire Grambling team turned to cover the punt.

"The whole field opened up," Billings said. "He could have walked to the end zone."

But Stancil, mindful of Collick's weeklong admonishment to get the first down sprinted straight for the first down marker. When he got there and stepped out of bounds, Collick exploded.

"What in the hell are you doing?" Collick unloaded.

"You told me to get the first down," Stancil sputtered. "You've been telling me that all week in practice."

Billings arrived on the scene and tried to calm the normally stoic head coach. "All he did was what you've been telling him to do," Billings said. "He got the first down. Let's go!"

A touchdown at the end of the third quarter and a field goal in the fourth closed Del State to within 35-31. But a Grambling touchdown with under five minutes to play extended the lead back to 11. Yet, Del State answered with a touchdown and then recovered an onside kick. With less than two minutes to play, they had the ball and a chance at the win. The Hornets quickly moved to the 16-yard line and with :49 left Billings sent in a play. It was his now his turn to lose his cool.

"Erik Jones was our quarterback and he came to the line of scrimmage and checked out of it," Billings said. "I'm on the sidelines yelling at him and going crazy and the play he calls is a sweep for Phil Anderson ... who goes for a 16-yard touchdown."

The Hornets added a two-point conversion and held on to win the game, 45-42 … thanks to a fake punt, an onside kick, and a last-minute audible. The loss was one of only two Grambling would have in 1992.

"It was one of those nights," Billings said. "Everything we tried worked."

The on-field celebration rivaled the party from almost a decade earlier at Florida A&M (minus the sprinklers). Players and their family members who had found their way onto the field laughed and danced with the Delaware State band. Several players sat at midfield and gaped at the dome above them.

"I've been watching you," Robinson told Collick after the game. "I've seen what you've done there. It's very commendable."

Later, at the airport, Robinson and Collick sat together while waiting for their flights home. Robinson regaled the Hornets' coach with tales from his 50 years in coaching.

"I always wanted to be a coach," Robinson said. "When I was a little kid I used to listen to the Rose Bowl on the radio and I'd dream of coaching in a game that big."

Collick enjoyed relating a Robinson story about being in class in second grade when the teacher said every student had to stand up and say what they wanted to be when they grew up. Robinson made the mistake of telling a girl in front of him that he wanted to be a football coach. When it was the girl's turn to speak she told the teacher, "I'm not sure what I want to do but that big kid behind me wants to be a football coach."

Robinson laughed as he lamented to Collick that he never even got the chance to tell the class what he wanted to do. Wanting to be a coach and actually becoming one, particularly for a young black man in 1941, were two different things. After graduating from Leland College, Robinson got a job for 25 cents an hour in a feed mill. He heard that the Louisiana Negro Normal and Industrial Institute (renamed Grambling in 1946) needed a coach. He convinced the school's president to hire him with a pledge that he'd take care of everything: He would line the fields, tape the players' ankles, and make sure they went to class.

"I was a sharecroppers' son and I got this opportunity thanks to an education," Robinson said to Collick. "Only in America can people like us, who come from certain situations, rise above those situations and live a better life. All because of education."

The two discussed that last point. Collick was with Robinson in the belief that education was the entire point of the exercise. The football part was easy. Getting the education was harder and more important.

Collick asked Robinson about a story he had heard from former Grambling quarterback Doug Williams. Williams told Collick that if a player was sleeping in instead of going to class Robinson would sneak into the kid's room and bang a pot with a steel spoon above the player's head. Robinson laughed and indicated that it was true.

At another airport in another time Delaware State players and coaches sat sullenly and ignored strangers. Now, in the busy Detroit airport, the coach of the Hornets sat and laughed with one of the legends of college football after the Hornets had defeated him. Collick almost pinched himself to make sure it was all really happening.

"To get that win over Coach Robinson was bigger than getting a win over Grambling," McLaurin said. "It was a huge story within the Black College football community."

While Delaware State was pulling a rabbit out of the hat in Detroit, Purzycki was at home listening to the game on the radio and wearing a hole in the carpet in his living room.

He was out of coaching now. His six seasons at James Madison produced the Dukes first-ever trip to the NCAA playoffs in 1987, but he didn't win as often as he or the school's administration would like. In 1991 they agreed to part ways. He had dismissed Billings a year earlier, a decision that strained their friendship for years. The entire experience in Harrisonburg left him emotionally drained and willing to consider other career options. He had moved back to Delaware and taken a job in banking with MBNA in 1991 and would spend the rest of his working years building up a portfolio of successful work for various financial institutions.

But, on this day, he might as well have still been on the Del State sideline. He knew Collick and he knew Billings and had a pretty good idea what they were going to do on every play. He lived and died with each call, pumping his fist when something went right and agonizing over the things that went wrong.

He felt they were in it until the late Grambling TD and about the time he was resigning himself to a defeat stood and stared at the radio in slack-jawed amazement as Del State roared back for the improbable triumph. Purzycki is a man with the gift of reverie and when the game finished, he thought back to his first days on the Delaware State campus in the winter of 1981 when he set a goal for Delaware State football.

> *"The guys on my staff think Delaware State is a sleeping giant," he had said to the players who decided to stay with him. "I want you to have success. I want this place to be special. Guys, I want to make this place the Grambling of the East."*

On September 26, 1992, the Delaware State Hornets were good enough to be on the same field with Grambling, good enough to beat Grambling in that game, and good enough based on what Collick had accomplished in Purzycki's wake to have reached what once seemed like an outlandish goal.

"Dream deferred. Dream realized." Purzycki thought to himself. "Delaware State is the Grambling of the East."

THIRTY-TWO

"The worst sin towards our fellow creatures is not to hate them, but to be indifferent to them; that's the essence of inhumanity."

– George Bernard Shaw

We're all looking for some sort of validation, something that makes us feel like we matter as humans. But we also come to expect basic recognition in our day to day lives. I am somebody.

When we apply for a job, we want to be taken seriously. When we walk into a restaurant, we expect to be served. On a street corner when hailing a cab, we expect one to stop. When we are looking for a home or an apartment, we expect to have a chance to buy it.

Like all of our best and worst human traits, there are many ways to play racism.

The overt acts, the acts of verbal, written or physical intimidation and hatred have been and unfortunately will be with us forever. There will always be people willing to shout a slur or paint a sign or attack someone solely based on their skin color, heritage, or religion. There will always be people who are willing to hate.

Another way racism can be played is more subtle but no less confounding. It's when a person chooses to *ignore* another person because of skin color, heritage, or religion. It's when an employer or landlord doesn't treat a job or apartment applicant fairly, a waiter snubs a diner, a cab won't stop to pick up a fare. This kind of thing happens every day and is one of the true essences of the frustration often felt by people of color.

In his first months in Dover, Joe Purzycki was the target of protests and hateful propaganda. His office was vandalized. People in positions of power tried to influence his players in a negative and openly hostile effort meant to undermine his chances for success.

But he also saw and felt what it was like to be ignored. He'd walk across campus, see a student he knew from his days as a coach at Caesar Rodney High School, and then feel his heart sink as the student quickly averted his gaze and walked the other direction. He spent much of his time alone because people couldn't or wouldn't speak to him.

Coincidentally, his team was in the same boat, and that's one of the first things they had in common. Delaware State football at the end of 1980 had been beaten so thoroughly so often that many people on campus either overtly mocked them for their ineptitude or, worse still, ignored them.

Nelson Townsend felt that indifference and it was one of the reasons he hired Purzycki. He knew the reaction to the hiring might not be positive but decided concerns about that were outweighed by Purzycki's connections across the state of Delaware, the success he had enjoyed as a player and a coach, and his intimate knowledge of the University of Delaware program. Townsend wanted to hire the best man for the job and decided Purzycki was that man.

Purzycki was naïve to think he was going to be "just a football coach" at Del State, as he declared during his first press conference. And while Townsend wasn't trying to advance some social agenda with the hire, he may have been naïve in underestimating the rancor in response to hiring a white man to one of the most visible leadership positions at Delaware State. By the end of Purzycki's first day on the job, they both had a better understanding of how people felt about the move.

"We knew that this was not necessarily the hottest decision," Townsend said. "We were plowing fertile ground, virgin ground."

"He had a lot of players upset with him because they didn't want a white coach," Terry Staples said. "There were a lot of unhappy people. Alumni, particularly football alumni, couldn't understand why Townsend couldn't find a black coach who was qualified."

As those early days unfolded and Purzycki and Townsend sometimes found themselves on the receiving end of the worst of human behavior, Townsend's respect and admiration for his new coach increased. He had endured that kind of crap longer and more often than Purzycki ever would and recognized that just because the hatred and ignorance were traveling in an unusual direction didn't mean it stung any less to the recipient.

"Prejudice flows in all directions," Townsend told author Brian Curtis in 2005. "No matter who you are, if you're a victim of prejudice the feeling is not a comfortable one."

So, Purzycki and Townsend and those who stepped in behind them began a fight on two fronts in January of 1981. Purzycki had to convince a skeptical community that he was, in fact, just a football coach. There was no agenda to usurp Delaware State College into a satellite campus of the University of Delaware. There was no plan to disrespect or dishonor the history and passion people had for HBCUs or to recruit primarily white players.

He had been hired to bring order to a football program in chaos and that was the other part of this story. When they were done, after Purzycki's four years and Bill Collick's ensuing run of success, they had not only brought order but a level of unprecedented success to a program that had been virtually invisible. With Townsend's unshakable support, Purzycki, his staff, and the players created a culture that made it impossible for people to continue to be indifferent about Delaware State football.

Years later, they all realize they were part of a something extraordinary and while their opinions differ on the importance of various incidents that happened along the way they are united in the belief they shared a very unique journey.

"It was us against the world, and the world was everybody," said Frank Burton, one of Purzycki's first recruits. "Administration, the community, all the teams we played. And the 'us' was all of us: the players, the coaching staff. We knew we were coming to a team that was a laughingstock. We were going to do whatever we could do to lift each other up on and off the field, so we could all excel. We were different, and we knew it."

Upperclassmen at Delaware State tried to influence Burton when he arrived as a freshman to be against Purzycki, but he told them pointedly that he was going to make up his own mind.

"He was a trailblazer going against the grain, but he wasn't trying to prove a point or stir up a commotion," Burton said of the coach. "He believed he was the best person for the job, he thought he was equipped and capable. He didn't just talk about it. He had a vision for what we could become."

Running back Steven Holiday was also in Purzycki's first recruiting class and came to admire Townsend's willingness to hire him in the first place.

"It was a very impressive move and it took a lot of heart and guts for him to do that," Holiday said. "Mr. Townsend hired the best man for the job and in a lot of cases back then, and still today, people in positions of power don't do that. They try to hire the right fit and that disturbs me a lot. HBCUs are always cognizant of maintaining their heritage and their culture and in *that* respect, Joe wasn't the best fit for the job. But he was the best guy."

"Nelson took more heat than anyone, but he made it clear to us that he wasn't worried about stepping out on a limb," assistant coach Greg McLaurin said. "We were at the very end of the civil rights movement and it took some gumption to hire Joe for the position."

"Mr. Townsend totally thought out of the box on the coaching decision," Thunder Thornton agreed. "More often than not we become too comfortable with taking the easy road. Doing something different, something that was not cookie cutter, was great. It was the turning point for the program."

Calvin Mason was against the hiring at first and was one of the original people who organized protests. But as he saw the organization and passion Purzycki and his staff brought to the team, he became convinced that the hire was a good one.

"Mr. Townsend was very smart, and he knew how to find the right people," Mason said. "I talked to him about what was going on and found out that this wasn't just stuff he was throwing together. He had a plan for what we could do to make the program better."

"He had a great mind for the job," Diane Townsend said. "He could see the whole picture; where you were, where you wanted to go, and all the moves you had to make. It was like a chess game to him and he could see all the pieces and parts you needed to reach your goal."

"Nelson had Dr. Mishoe's ear and he had great vision," Bill Collick said. "He had seen success in black college football and he thought we could do that at Delaware State."

Calvin Stephens never played a down for Purzycki. By 1981 his football career at Delaware State was over and he was preparing to graduate. But he was a thoughtful observer who quickly concluded that Purzycki's hiring and the buzz surrounding it could be good for the Hornets.

"The old saying don't judge a book by its cover… early on people were judging Coach Purzycki by his cover instead of as a person," Stephens said. "A lot of times in life we see and think stuff and we have a different perception, without really knowing. We were a black college. Weren't we supposed to have a black coach? No. That shouldn't even play into the equation."

Linebacker Mike Colbert was already on campus when Purzycki arrived and in retrospect thinks some of the pushback from students and players to Purzycki's hiring was a natural extension not only of the pride students had in Del State being an HBCU, but also because they were college students.

"That whole thing when you're in college – about rebellion, that was initially the feeling on campus," Colbert said. "We understood how some of the players and community felt about this white man because there were other qualified candidates who were African American."

Purzycki was able to win the team over due primarily to three things: he was authentic, he had a vision for the program, and he was a spectacular orator.

"When I got to Delaware State I made the conscious decision to use figures who young African Americans could relate to when I was trying to provide motivation and inspiration for our young men," Purzycki said. He patterned his speaking style after two men who had been idols to him growing up, John Kennedy and Martin Luther King. "They both spoke with a rhythm and a cadence that kept people spellbound."

Purzycki regaled his team with stories about Wilma Rudolph overcoming numerous childhood diseases to become a great Olympian, Jesse Owens winning gold in Germany in front of Hitler, Sarah Breedlove Walker, who was born two years after the Civil War ended and developed a line of cosmetics for African-American women. She is acknowledged as the first female self-made millionaire in American history. He told stories about Rafer Johnson, Muhammad Ali, and Bill Russell.

"I wanted these young men to know I respected them, and where they came from." Purzycki also studied old African proverbs and used them to make points. His favorite one: "If you want to go fast, go alone. If you want to go far, go together."

It can be tricky for a white man to use black history in an attempt to motivate a team that was 95 percent black players. But Purzycki made it work because of his authenticity.

"His honesty won the hearts of a lot of people," Diane Townsend said. "He had a great attitude, he was considerate, and he was loving towards his players. When people would see that, it would change their minds. All of those things coming together is what brought fans in and once they were in, they liked Joe."

"If you didn't do your background work and you didn't know anything about him it was easy to make a quick assessment," Burton said. "But if you listened to him and understood his story you found out he grew up in the city of Newark. He had dealt with African Americans and Hispanics growing up."

"That Newark upbringing helped him," Joe Lane agreed. "That helped him a lot because he knew how to talk to us. The way he quoted Dr. King and the others, you could tell it was coming from a place in his heart."

"Joe wasn't a guy who grew up in a rich, affluent neighborhood," Matt Horace said. "He wasn't that guy who had never been around diversity and never been around hardship. He would tell guys in practice, 'I know where you come from in Philadelphia. I know where you come from in Newark.' Or Baltimore, or D.C., or New York.' He connected in that way for the people who were willing to listen."

Because he had that background, because he knew what it was like to spend a year at college and then return to your neighborhood,

Horace said he also could speak with authority to his players about avoiding potential pitfalls.

"He'd tell us, 'Every time you go home you'll see guys on the corner drinking, playing dice, involved in drugs and gangs. You'll see all kinds of people not moving the same way you're moving.' He'd remind us that we were college athletes playing the game we loved with people we loved," Horace related. "He always told us not to waste our time, to take advantage of the opportunity we had. He said that all the time."

"I never met anyone in coaching or business who motivated me more," Thornton said.

"Purzycki was great at explaining his vision for the program," Colbert said. "Coach Collick and Coach Purzycki were always talking about what we were building. 'You guys are going to remember this! You're going to remember that you built the foundation at Delaware State!' That was profound, and based on what he and Collick did, he was absolutely right."

"I look back and I know we had a hand in that," said Walt Samuels, who played for Purzycki in 1981, "and I'm very proud of that."

"Delaware State football stood tall for a long time," echoed Colbert.

"They were just getting crushed," Holliday said, "and he changed the landscape of the entire program."

One of the recurring themes Purzycki used in building buy-in among his players was a reminder that they had all been overlooked in some way. That was an easy sell to his players because it was true. Most of them had ended up at Delaware State after something somewhere else didn't work out.

"It was not a destination, it was an accident if you were there," Franz Kappel said. "Nobody wanted to come there. Kid after kid at Del State had something against them but we came here and found a place."

"We were all fringe players," said Dan Candeloro. "We weren't tall enough, or fast enough or big enough. We always joked that we were the island of misfit toys."

"But Purzycki convinced us all to give it a chance," Kappel said. "He got us to work together, and stay together, and he instilled a pride in Delaware State in all of us."

Lane thinks the ramifications of Purzycki's hiring rippled out of Dover and spread around the conference. Many in the MEAC worried that if a white coach had success at one of their schools then other schools would follow suit. But that's not what happened when the Hornets starting winning.

"Purzycki's success helped change the culture of the MEAC," Lane said. "Everything changed. Teams stepped up and hired better coaches; travel got better."

Delaware State getting good meant everyone else had to get a little better.

"What we were, and what we became in just a couple years, was incredible," Staples said. "We were so far behind every other program. We didn't have a weight room, we had no tradition, we had nothing. It all had to be built. Just to get us level with the other teams was a big accomplishment."

Billings, Collick, and Purzycki view the story from unique perspectives.

Billings studied the Bible more often in his later years and came to view what happened at Delaware State and his role in it from a spiritual viewpoint.

"I'm not that religious, but I'm getting better at it," Billings said. "I've done enough sinning for two people. I was at a meeting with some people from a church and the preacher was talking about when God came down and appeared to Moses as a burning bush to tell him that he needed Moses to take care of his people.

"Moses is like, 'Wait a minute. I'm not so sure about this. You've gotta pick the right guy for this job.' The preacher pointed out that Moses was the right guy for the job and then he asked us all, 'What is *your* burning bush. How will you know it when you see it?'"

"Here's how," Billings continued as his voice shook with emotion. "If the purpose is from God it will always honor God, bless other people, and bring you joy. That's what Del State is to me. It was *my* burning bush; I thought we changed an image. We were working on more than football here. The whole school was humiliated by that loss to Portland. And we heard it all. 'Black kids won't get the Wing-T. You can't win at Del State. You'll never get the support necessary for long-term success.' We proved them wrong. We brought respectability and wins to that school. It was really an undertaking, and it was fun."

Collick is proud of the success they all enjoyed on the football field but his primary source of satisfaction from his time at Delaware State involves the number of young people he helped to get an education. Carl Collick's nephew never forgot the immense pride he and his family felt for his uncle who was the first in the Collick family to attend college. His uncle spoke to him right after he was named to replace Purzycki as Del State's head coach.

"He was so elated," Collick remembered. "He was so proud of me and told me to never lose sight of what my calling was, to give as many young men as possible the same opportunity he had received. He felt so good about where I was and what I was doing."

Collick took special pleasure in players he recruited who were first in their family to get that chance.

"I loved watching them arrive on that first day," Collick said. "They would be there with their mom and dad, maybe their grandparents, uncles, and aunts, sometimes a family minister, and the whole group was so proud of the young man who was entering college. They were all looking for a better way of life.

"I gave kids a chance to get in the game. Higher education elevates you and to be a part of that was so special. When I look back on that deal, how could I do any better?"

For Purzycki, it was a transcendent four years that dramatically impacted his entire life.

"My Delaware State experience is my most important in all of my years," Purzycki said. "I have been a successful coach and I have been an executive at some of the biggest companies in the world. I have been a COO and vice chairman at one of those companies. But the greatest experience of my professional life, by far, came at a tiny Historically Black College in Dover, Delaware."

The story is further enhanced by a look at the MEAC Athletics Hall of Fame. Since its inception in 1981, the highly selective organization has only inducted 143 people and just five of those came from Delaware State. All five men, Dr. Luna Mishoe, Nelson Townsend, Bill Collick, Gene Lake, and John Taylor had direct ties to those first two Purzycki seasons.

Nelson Townsend died in early 2015 at the age of 73. He had just been named the athletic director at Florida A&M and was in the early days of his third tenure as the Rattlers' AD when he suffered a heart attack.

Diane Townsend said her husband knew he would raise a lot of eyebrows when he decided to hire Purzycki. But the same guy who didn't worry about who got the credit was willing to take the heat for something he thought would put Delaware State on the best path to success.

"Nelson was looking for something different," she said. "He loved what they were doing at Delaware. He was a big fan of the Wing-T and thought it was an offense our guys could run. But he understood the fear other people had. For higher level educators the black college was all we had, and many people felt we had to keep it that way. Some people thought that by hiring Joe he was giving all that away.

"But he just wanted the program to be in the best place. Sometimes, the university had some thought on where they wanted to go but they weren't always willing to do all the stuff they needed to do to get to that point.

"Some people start with good intentions but then they hear people around them saying negative things they become afraid of the potential results of a tough decision. That's a battle you have to want to fight and the only way to fight it is to do it."

Townsend and Purzycki engaged in that fight with equal parts courage, knowledge, guts, and humor. By the end of day one, which dramatically lurched off course in every conceivable way, they both realized the fight was going to be even tougher than they could have anticipated, yet each man was willing to push his entire stack of chips into the center of the table.

Mr. Townsend and the Polish Prince were all in, critics be damned.

Jeff Cannon might have summed it up best. The low-key coach responsible for an offensive line that made the Hornets' running game borderline unstoppable in 1983 and '84 often preached to his players and fellow coaches on the virtues and attainable goals available to those who choose to row in the same direction.

"We are better off when we focus more on what we have in common than that which divides us."

When Purzycki first took the job at Delaware State, his brother Mike shared with him a story he had heard from decathlete Bob

Mathias. Mathias won the gold medal in the event at the Olympics in 1948 and 1952. Fellow American Milt Campbell won the silver medal in 1952 and in 1956 he became the first African American to win gold in the decathlon. Rafer Johnson won silver in 1956 and then won the gold medal in 1960 becoming the second African American to do so.

The three men formed a close bond over the years and Mathias was once asked what he learned about competing against Campbell and Johnson.

Mathias pointed out that the Big Top is the largest tent at a circus and that in that tent there is always a net covering thousands of helium-filled balloons of every color. Once released the balloons all rise and the circus begins.

"What I learned from Rafer and Milt," Mathias said, "was that if you filled the black and the brown balloons with the same amount of helium as the white, red and yellow balloons, they would rise to the top of the big tent like all the others."

Purzycki often uses Mathias' story in speeches as a way of describing what he learned from Nelson Townsend and the players who played for him at Delaware State College from 1981 to 1984. Many of those players were in attendance at a banquet in 2005 when Purzycki was inducted into the Delaware Afro-American Sports Hall of Fame (Collick was inducted in 2004). During his speech that night, he said it was the players who were deserving of recognition and praised them for having the courage to stick with him when so many urged them not to.

"What was built at Delaware State is remarkable," Purzycki said. "From the bedrock of despair and failure came 13 consecutive winning seasons, an outstanding graduation rate, and five MEAC championships. It was all started by that group of guys who hung in there with us in 1981 and 1982. Young and old, black and white, city guys and country kids, they all came together during the tough times. This is their legacy. And at the top was Nelson, who had my back in the worst of times."

When Nelson Townsend made the decision to hire Joe Purzycki he didn't expect the widespread dramatic reaction. As the years passed, he came to appreciate what had transpired in Dover, Delaware, in the early 1980s.

"Nelson really did not know the impact it would have on the school, the community, and HBCU history," Diane Townsend said. "He had no idea that bringing Purzycki in would create so much controversy. He never thought about it or spoke about it. He didn't know it would be seen as history. But that's what it was.

"It was sports history in a small little place."

ACKNOWLEDGEMENTS

The telling of a story nearly 40 years old required a great deal of assistance and would not have been possible without the terrific reporting of Scott Wasser, Steve Adamek, Jerry McGuire, and John Millman of the *Delaware State News*.

In particular, thanks to Scott Wasser for taking the time to go over details of the events in Dover in early 1981.

Important knowledge of the story was also gained thanks to the great work of Jack Ireland, Gene Bryson, Jack Chevalier, Matt Zabitka, and Tom Tomashek of the *Wilmington News Journal*.

In addition, thanks to author Brian Curtis whose initial online story about Joe and Nelson in 2006 served as a great resource. Brian graciously shared his notes and thoughts from his work. I am grateful for his assistance.

Thanks to Chuck Newman of the Philadelphia Inquirer.

Thanks to Don Borst. A story that combines football and social issues needed an editor who is passionate and knowledgeable about both. I'm grateful you took on the challenge.

Thanks to Rejoice Scherry, the University Archivist and Special Collections Librarian at Delaware State University.

Thanks to the 1981 staff at the *Hornet*. Your colorful reporting reflected the mood of the students at Delaware State.

Thanks to everyone at the Delaware Public Archives at the state capitol in Dover.

Thanks to the players who were generous with time and enthusiasm for this project. Matt Horace, Thunder Thornton, Calvin Mason, Anthony Sharpe, Walt Samuels, Terry Staples, Calvin Stephens, Mike Colbert, Sam Warren, Bobby Swoope, Ace Comer, Steve Holiday, Frank Burton, Joe Lane, Franz Kappel, Nigel Dunn, Richard Williams, John Taylor, James Niblack, and Dan Candeloro.

Several other players are quoted and mentioned in the book. These quotes came primarily from newspaper stories. Thanks to them and to all the Hornets.

This story benefitted mightily from the time, wit, and wisdom given to me by Bill Collick and Herky Billings.

It was a delight spending time with Diane Townsend. At the end of one of our conversations, I told her that all the stories she shared with me about Nelson allowed me to feel like I knew him. "Well," she replied, "he was a man who was worth knowing." He sure was. Thanks, Diane.

Thanks to Greg McLaurin, Allen Hamilton, and David Fargnoli. Your memories helped fill in some important blank spots.

Thanks to Matt Urban and the team at NuPoint Marketing in Wilmington and to Brent Swenson at Rhombus in Seattle.

Thanks to Les McCarthy of Pathfinder Publications.

Thanks to Sharon Purzycki for your hospitality and the details you contributed.

Finally, thanks to Joe Purzycki. The first time I heard these stories was on long road trips with the James Madison University football team. You said then that someone should write a book about your time at Delaware State. Thanks for choosing me to do it.

Photo Credits:
Delaware State University library
Delaware State University sports information department
Gary Emeigh
Personal collection of Joe Purzycki

For more information on Delaware State University athletics go to Dsuhornets.com.

For more information on the people in Mr. Townsend and the Polish Prince go to thepolishprince.com.

For more information on Mike Gastineau go to gasman206.com.

Made in the USA
Middletown, DE
07 March 2019